INTO ME SEE

A Book for Daily Inspiration

KAREN S. WYLIE, M.A.

Oct. 2015

Dear Barbara,

How wonderful to spend sacred time with you. May these words always remind you of the wholeness, perfection and love within!

Blessings,
Karen

Cover design by Joyce Huntington

ISBN-13: 978-1508531036

This book is dedicated to all Seekers of Truth.

May you continue to ask the tough questions.

It's All Sacred!

If God said, Rumi, pay homage to everything
that has helped you enter my arms, there
would not be one experience of my life, not
one thought, not one feeling, not any act, I
would not bow to.
Jalaludin Rumi (1207-1273)

What I've come to realize is that everything
that has ever happened to me throughout
my entire life has been sacred — all that has
been joyful and all that has caused me pain.

INTRODUCTION

Dearest Readers,

I want to call you "Beings of Light" for that is what you are whether you know it or not.

The following reflections were written by me over the course of the last sixteen years, which has been a most important period in my life as it has been a time of great spiritual growth and expansion. These writings appeared in various monthly editions of the Inner Visions magazine published by the Agape International Spiritual Center in Culver City over the period from 1998 to 2014.

This is a book about answers—at least the answers which have served me as one who has always asked a lot of questions. Because of that, it holds a very special place in my heart. That should not be too surprising. What these 16 years and all these writings reveal to me is that we are in school, the Learning Laboratory of Life 101. We are constantly learning new lessons (or not). School is always in session. The good news is that this loving universe provides as many opportunities as we need to learn the lesson we've come here to learn. What we miss today will come again tomorrow. When we become ready for the next lesson, it appears. I am clearly a student, like you, and I suspect I will be until the end of my physical life and beyond.

As I was dealing with various issues in my own life, struggling with some personal challenge, upon meditation and contemplation, answers would come to me as timely revelations that would always bring peace into my own heart. The best writings always resulted from my learning the biggest lessons, and they were part of my own self-discovery.

My simple hope is that these writings will be helpful to you. You might use them as daily inspiration, something to think about and ponder, or meditate upon, as you begin each new day.

What I now believe with certainty is that we do live in a loving, supportive universe. If there is a desire in your heart to know anything, the answer will be revealed. May you experience much joy and happiness on your own soul journey!

In peace and love, Karen Wylie

I am so grateful to offer these writings for your contemplation and spiritual inspiration. Throughout this book, I'm following a format used in several spiritual publications. I begin each piece with a quote that inspired me and I hope will inspire you. If you are touched by the writers and spiritual books I've chosen, I urge you to search out these sources of inspiration.

Spend some time with each piece. This is not a book to rush through! I would suggest you have the book by your bedside to read in the morning or at night... just a little bit, followed by some time to digest and reflect on what you have read.

The positive affirmation at the end of each piece is my special gift to you. I urge you to repeat it to yourself throughout the day, as a reminder of the power that lies within you.

You are a beautiful, radiant being of light. May my writing inspire you to remember who you are.

Beings of Light

It is a fact of the Universe that you are a Being in formation. You do not need to bring any other "information" except what you are to the process of Life in order for what you are to be made manifest in form. You merely need to allow the process of formation to take place in its own way, in its own time.

Neale Donald Walsch, *Bringers of the Light*

On one level, nothing remains the same. On another level, I feel the assured constancy of the Love of God that is always the same. I have discovered that I am not a noun. I am a verb. I am Being—a pure expression of Divine Spirit.

The absolute truth about your nature and being is that you are spiritually made in the image and likeness of God. The larger part of you has never been hurt, harmed or endangered in any way. Who you really are is always ready to shine as the infinite possibility of your true destiny of greatness. Nothing stops us from infinite expression in all areas of our lives except our inability to embody the totality of who and what we are.

Regardless of what you have experienced in the past or are experiencing now, the larger part of you lives in infinite love, peace, joy, abundance, wisdom and truth—you name it—and is just awaiting your own realization of it. In that, you shall be made brand new. How freeing it is to "let loose" the tight bands that have been restricting you. You do not need to hold back. There is nothing you have to protect against. When you consciously and consistently attune yourself to the living Spirit within you, you are set free to live and love fearlessly with an undefended heart!

Affirmation:

I embrace the truth that I am the Infinite Life of God expressing throughout eternity. I live in the joy of my Being!

Love, the Absence of Fear

Learn to think about what you wish to become.

Ernest Holmes, *This Thing Called Life*

Love alone can overcome fear because love surrenders itself to the object of its adoration.

Ernest Holmes, *The Science of Mind*

What I see when I don't see love is simply fear. It can appear in the disguise of anger, pain, lack, hurt feelings, aggression or violence of all kinds, including war; but at its core, it is fear.

Ernest Holmes says fear is the great enemy of man. That is our constant challenge—to transmute fear into faith—faith in a benevolent, all-inclusive, giving universe, which is the truth. It is about choice. We always have the choice to choose the light over the darkness.

Sometimes we can be so overcome by our fear that we think there is a powerful force of evil behind it that holds us captive, but that is not the truth. Love is the most powerful force in the world. Love conquers all. Just a shift in thinking, taking fear into faith and believing you are loved, protected and guided by a benevolent universe can turn a life of hell into one of bliss.

God is available not only to some of us. God is available to all of us. We are all the chosen ones as long as we choose God. Faith is the answer. Love is the answer. How wonderful to know that we are the beloved in whom God is well pleased. The kingdom of God is available to us here on earth; all we have to do is say "yes" to it, and our very world is transformed before our eyes.

Affirmation:

I know that the spirit of the living God goes before me and makes perfect my way. I rest in calm peace and in absolute certainty that all the good there is, is devoted to my well-being.

Trust Love

The rhythm of my heart is the birth and death of all that is alive.

Thich Nhat Hanh

Every soul is a celestial Venus to every other soul... Love is our highest word, and the synonym of God.

Ralph Waldo Emerson

How can we trust again when our love has been betrayed? How can we dare to feel again? I say how can we not? I realize when I don't trust love with another, it is me I am denying. How can I deny love to this one whom I hold so dear? How can I deny love to this one who is the cherished blessing of God?

Whatever story you have told of your life, the story is over. You can declare this moment the beginning of your life. You are not a victim of your circumstances. You have choice. The gift that is given to all of us is the ability to change our minds. Yes, it does take some effort to retrain the mind. We have spent our lifetime entertaining faulty thoughts. We struggled to make sure that we were in control as part of our survival technique. That very need to control keeps us now from our freedom. We see that we can only have what we are willing to give away to others. We make room in our hearts for more each time we give away what we really want.

In a new state of awareness, we become the observer. We simply observe our thoughts, not making ourselves bad or wrong for them—and in an instant, we can choose to change our mind, always being gentle with the self.

It is time to surrender to the truth of your being. You are indeed infinite love expressing everywhere!

Affirmation:

I am the radiant presence of God. Nothing can keep me from my good. I love in the awareness of divine perfection. I trust love for I am the love that I seek.

Care of the Soul

To enter the sacred chamber of the soul is to find the answer to every prayer, the long sought fulfillment of every heart's desire; whatever the soul has longed for, the same will be found in this inner sanctuary of eternal life; and the path has been called the silence.

Christian D. Larson, *The Pathway of Roses*

I was born for the nurturing of my soul. It is in the nurturing of my soul that I am set free. It hungers for love, beauty and peace. The love my soul seeks is unconditional in its nature. It does not desire to control or manipulate. It is defenseless and genuine.

As the weight of my life's story (that which I thought defined me) has been lifted off me, I am able to awaken to my soul's desires. It is not confused by the demands of the outer world for it is pure in its longing, and it is self-directing when I listen. It provides what it seeks—that which was there all the time. It experiences infinite abundance because what it seeks cannot be bought. I see that my soul is my salvation. Everything else is transitory. The soul is unchanging in its nature.

I care for it by listening to its desires. I give it time each day— special time. I sit quietly with it while it speaks to me. It reveals all of life to me for it is wise beyond measure. Its ancient wisdom sources me, enabling me to see through the illusion of my limited perception. In the quiet, it comforts me and I feel its love enfolding me. It is in the quiet that I remember who I am. What I experience in the silence carries over more and more into all of my day, enabling me to capture a thousand beautiful moments that I otherwise would not have known. I experience joy over the smallest things because I understand their relevance.

I've grown to love the quiet time for its revelations of love, beauty, peace and truth. It has made me strong and resilient; and I realize that in the quiet, I am home.

Affirmation:

I honor my soul's longing for itself. In the silence, I experience my true nature. I do not struggle or resist anything for I see that I am everything.

Eternal Expansion

The perfected man... does not interfere in the life of beings; he does not impose himself on them, but he helps all beings to their freedom (Lao-tse). Through his unity, he leads them too, to unity; he liberates their nature and their destiny; he releases Tao in them.

M. Buber, *Pointing the Way*

It is not always easy to let go of the familiar, to let go of places, people and ideas that no longer serve us. It is, however, what happens as the consciousness is up leveled. As we surrender our small will into the will of God, which is infinite, our small life transforms.

We cannot know precisely what is coming next because we are no longer orchestrating the details. We have the vision—it is important to have the vision—but we do not need to know the "how." The "how" is a pleasant surprise—pleasant because we are always up leveling to the greater, not the lesser. We become more fearless because we see the way being made smooth before us. We see that we are protected and indeed so loved by that invisible something which propels our journey.

We are on course. We are living in higher awareness all the time, so that even our times of doubting become shorter in duration. We hang out in the space of complete surrender and faith in the invisible something.

There is this awakened knowledge that we are truly here to be the divine servant. We see what an honored privilege it is that there is no higher expression in the human form, and we are blessed beyond our own understanding.

This is the life of the devoted one. Assuredly, this is not a life of deprivation and lack. This is truly a life of limitless abundance in all areas. We are here to be more, to know more, to give more and to love more.

Affirmation:

I surrender myself into my greatness! I'm willing to be shown the way. I rest in the awareness of the love which surrounds me! I am the living expression of the one and only.

Passionate Living

Today... I focus my energy on love, appreciation, and my highest possibilities. Today I claim responsibility for my own success, and step forward with a new enthusiasm to manifest unprecedented good. I use my mind to create only the best, and I draw unto me all the support and resources I need for positive change.

Alan Cohen, *Handle with Prayer*

Living in spirit is passionate living. Passionate living is living in excitement and enthusiasm for the surprise of each moment. Do you believe that you can live at this level of awareness and not be passionate? It is not possible. The vibrancy of life is so rich and full and heart opening. The intricacies of life are not lost on one who loves God. No, instead there is beauty unbounded which touches the very core of one's being. Hence, even the most common of experiences can touch that place in us we know as God and create a new reality each and every day. By loving God, you lose nothing. Instead, you gain the world! Passionate living is bold living! It is unbounded living! It is fearless living! It is living in the awareness that all of God's kingdom is available to you.

As you let go of the persona of limited thinking and step into the surrendered state of true devotion, the world opens before you. The ego may continue its struggle for control all the while, filling you with fear thoughts. The greater the ego, the greater the fear, but there is that within you which cannot be defeated.

We are here to remember our true identity, to step into our greatness— to let go and truly surrender. Ironically, you do not surrender into weakness. You surrender into your greatest power.

How great thou art, Almighty Spirit, which creates out of itself such magnificence, such joy, such love! I live in the awareness of the cherished blessing of my life, knowing that I am here to fulfill God's divine idea as me, and I am set free!

Affirmation:

I radiate the love of God everywhere! I bask in the awareness of my true nature. I am the Beloved!

The Holy Instant

Nothing real can be threatened. Nothing unreal exists. Herein lies the peace of God.

Revelation is literally unspeakable because it is an experience of unspeakable love.

A Course in Miracles

While working with others in a class process, I experienced what I would call a holy instant. My soul was met by another through an exchange between us and I saw with profound clarity my absolute Oneness with another human being. In that instant, my Oneness with him and all creation was all that I could feel, see and know. Something within me was awakened, and I was called to a higher standard. What I heard through that exchange was that I was to love the unlovable and forgive the unforgivable. I realized that he was a messenger.

This phrase has been speaking to me since that moment. Spiritually, we are all lovable and forgivable, so what was the meaning here? I understand now that it is about being human. I see that it is easy to love the lovable and forgive the forgivable. The real test of devotion is this: Can we love what we would ignore or avoid or look away from? Can we look into the eyes of the homeless man on the street and truly love him? Can we love the one we think ruined our life?

Can we look into her eyes and see love? Can we love the irritating, passive-aggressive one the whole office dumps its abuse upon? Can we look into her eyes and really love her? Can we love the child molester or the one we have no use for?

Are we willing to go that deep? Something happens when we go that deep. The fear of differences and the suspicion of separation are gone, absolutely. We are at peace. We transcend the common idea of loving—we become the Love.

Today I am awake to choose differently. As I open my heart wider, my love expands and I become larger in my loving. I lose nothing in this, but gain everything. My soul meets and acknowledges itself in all others. I am willing to fully express all the love that I am! I want to be more loving in my heart. I am willing to be more loving in my heart!

Affirmation:

I am free to create a holy instant now. Today I choose an adventure in holy instants.

The Miracle Worker

Miracle working entails a full realization of the power of thought in order to avoid miscreation. The miracle worker must have genuine respect for true cause and effect as a necessary condition for the miracle to occur.

A Course in Miracles

You are the creator of your reality in every moment. Through that creation, you are experiencing heaven or hell here in physical form. The way you are creating is through your thought. It is not the words you speak but the energy behind your thoughts. So you can speak an affirmation, but if you are speaking from a place of lack, the lack is what you will be bringing into your life. This is the Law of Attraction. You bring into your life that which you focus upon, even when you are focusing on what you do not want. That is why we say you must not only talk the talk, you must walk the walk.

How do we walk the walk? How do we transform the energy behind the thought so that we truly begin to create our experience from love instead of fear? That is an inside job. It cannot be done ultimately by just exterior processes, though those processes help. It is done through your willingness to open up to the inner recesses of your being where you tap into universal intelligence or the Holy Spirit or God, or whatever you choose to call it. It is in that place that you begin to see that we live in a benevolent universe—a universe that is constantly giving, constantly providing for us. It is in that place that you begin to see that you are a co-creator with God and that every experience is one you have chosen, either consciously or unconsciously.

I call prayer and meditation the Holy Communion because it is how I've come to understand my connection to the whole. It is in that place that I've come to see that I am a powerful co-creator and that the world is for me, not against me. If anyone is against me, it is only me and my faulty thinking. This is good news because it means that anything is possible. Do you see the infinite possibility? I am in deep gratitude for this realization of my oneness with all of life. I continue to change my thinking so I can change my life!

Affirmation:

I claim my true identity now! I let go of my fear-thinking! I accept the love that is being poured forth into me now! I rejoice in my new reality!

Behold the Divine Self

When I have lost my way... when in loneliness I have sat in the thicket of despair too weak to move, to lift my head; Thou hast searched for and found me! I cannot escape Thy scrutiny! I would not escape Thy love!

Howard Thurman, *For the Inward Journey*

You cannot escape the love of God. You can deny God's love and God loves you in your denial. You can blame God or fear God, and God loves you in your fear and blame. You can ignore God, and God loves you in your ignorance. You can be angry at God and God loves you in your anger. This is the nature of unconditional love. It is for you to love yourself as God loves you. It is for you to see the blessed being that God sees—to see yourself with the eyes of God.

It is for you to let go of your self-condemnation and self-judgment. It is for you to behold the divine in yourself. When, with eyes cast inward, you can see the magnificence of your own being, you can then see that magnificence everywhere. As you open your heart to yourself you open your heart to others in a brand new way—not with the desire to get anything but instead with a desire to give of the love you are.

Perhaps you have not felt safe enough to open your heart—perhaps you have been afraid of being hurt. In that resistance, you bring to yourself the very hurt you would protect against. This is the moment to let go of all resistance. This is the moment to set yourself free. You cannot escape God's love! You cannot escape!

Affirmation:

I open my heart to the love I am! I am willing to see myself as God sees me! I let go of any resistance right now. I am set free!

False Identity Dissolved

Nothing outside yourself can save you; nothing outside yourself can give you peace.

A Course in Miracles

The ego-based life is lived from the outside in. It is lived in a false premise that the rewards come from the without, but rewards from the without are not lasting. The attainment of true joy and freedom is experienced when one is willing to live from the inside out.

One of the greatest challenges facing a seeker of truth is in the letting go of the ego's need to control and be seen. Instead of experiencing what is real without an agenda, the ego's business is about getting something for itself. Its purpose is to glorify itself and to maintain control because it is afraid. It is afraid to release its hold because it is filled with doubt. It exploits all situations in an attempt to get praise.

As egoic beings, we perceive through the filter of our life's story. In this way, each one's perception is different based on its history. As we surrender to the living spirit of the living God within us, we begin to see as God sees—not through the filter of confusion and fear; instead, we begin to see what is real and we cease to argue with it. We are brought to peace, to our salvation. We are humbled in our willingness to see as God sees because we realize at once that we are part of a vastness that is beyond our comprehension, a vastness which is infinite and complete in its nature.

Though the ego may continue its struggle for control, when we taste this freedom offered from our Inner Being, we cannot choose otherwise. We choose infinite life. We choose peace. In that, we find glory, but not from the without. We find glory from the within, and it is a lasting glory forever and ever!

Affirmation:

I let go of my faulty perception! I embrace the divine within me! I see who I am and I am set free!

Revelation of Spirit

My whole life is a revelation of Spirit! All of my relationships are sacred fellowship! I yield my small self to reveal my true self! My life is an adventure in insight! I surrender to God's big idea of my life! In all things I am grateful!

Affirmations from the Agape Revelation Conference 2000

Are you willing to love yourself unconditionally? Have you ever asked yourself this question? If you do, you might be surprised at the answer. Are you really willing to give yourself unconditional love, the kind of love that accepts everything there is about you—even what you would call your negative aspects? To the degree you would withhold love from yourself for some seeming imperfection, you judge and withhold it from your neighbor. What it means to love yourself unconditionally is to realize the kingdom of heaven within your own being.

Many times we want others to love us or respect us or honor us and we are unwilling to do that for ourselves. We are unwilling to forgive ourselves for events and circumstances of the past. It is important to forgive ourselves so that we can let go of the burden that weighs us down and makes us heavy and saps our energy. We lighten the load as we let go of judgments and move into forgiveness. We must find those disowned, unloved parts of ourselves and "bring them home" to our own unconditional loving.

As we integrate these disowned parts of ourselves back into that part of ourselves that I call the Divine Knower within, we become unified in our own internal unconditional loving and there ceases to be those negative aspects that get projected out onto others in our environment. Instead, we become a place for love to be expressed, seen and felt. We become a light-bearer. We become a safe haven. We become free from our need to judge and be judged.

Are you willing to love yourself unconditionally? Are you willing to set yourself free from your own self-condemnation and self-judgment? The truth is that your natural state is pure joy. You were born in bliss. As you lift these burdens that have weighed you down, you return to your original state of joy, and you are set free!

Affirmation:

I am willing to love myself unconditionally! I honor myself and see that my life is a revelation of Spirit! I yield my small self to reveal my true self! I surrender to God's big idea of my life!

Cosmic Selfhood

We interrupt what we are trying to become to have a realization of what we already are.

Michael Bernard Beckwith

Unless we are able to provide the consciousness, It (Spirit) cannot make the gift.

Ernest Holmes, *The Science of Mind*

So many of us are guilty of thinking that our good is somewhere out there in the future. I'll finally have it all as soon as I fix this one last thing. Rev. Michael's insight reminds us of the truth. Everything we need is already present.

"How can that be so?" you say. "I have no job. I can't pay my rent and my children are hungry." The minute you release your resistance to the idea that you are a powerful, magnificent co-creator with God, the job will appear, the rent money will show up and the children will be fed. "What resistance?" you say. "I constantly pray for a job and money to feed my children."

The resistance within you is a consciousness of poverty. It is from a consciousness of poverty that you are praying—from a belief that no matter what you do, nothing ever works out financially. The way to shift this consciousness into one of abundance is to begin to think and focus on the feeling tone of abundance and pray from that place. It may require you to write about the abundant life you desire, describing in detail the beautiful home you live in, the wonderful meal that you and your children are eating, the new job you have been offered, and other words that bring you into a feeling tone of abundance. Then, when you have captured that feeling tone and reside in it, pray in acceptance while you surrender in grace.

Nothing can keep you from experiencing the abundant flow of the universe except your resistance and thoughts about what you do not have. We live in a giving and sustaining universe that is perpetually working for us as we open our minds and hearts to it. Be willing to receive in the realization that you deserve the very best life has to offer as the divine being that you are!

Affirmation:

I am willing to receive the gifts of the kingdom! I open my mind and heart to the infinite idea of me! I'm rich in life and love! Nothing can keep me from my good!

Ushered Into the Light

The Soul is here for its own joy.

Rumi

There is a kind of rebirth that takes place for those of us on the spiritual path. We are being born of the Spirit. In our willingness, an opening is created and we are filled with living light. We become light beings; no more are we heavy with the burdens and misperceptions of a life lived in illusion. This happens as we let go, piece by piece, of the pain, suffering, unforgiveness, and misidentifications. Spirit moves into those dark places and they are ushered into the light. Along with the lightness of the body, we are suffused with an energy—a creative energy that is powerful in its force and nature. This is what it means to be reborn. Freedom is being born within us—freedom from ideas of lack and limitation and freedom from constricted thinking. We remember our true identity as sacred emanations of the Divine One.

This whole process begins with the simple willingness and desire to know more of God. It is available to all of us equally. There is no higher or lower among us. We are all divine beings in the sight of

God. There is no difference except in the degree of our individual willingness and desire.

As we remember who we were born to be, we let go of any false identification and we are suffused with love and joy which is our true nature. How wonderful to receive this gift of remembrance! My Soul sings in joy!

Affirmation:

My body is imbued with living light! I radiate infinite love and joy which is my true nature!

Choosing Peace

Because the human scene is entirely a misconception through misperception, any thought of helping, healing, correcting, or changing the material picture must be relinquished in order that we may see the ever-present reality.

Joel Goldsmith, *The Infinite Way*

Sometimes people in our lives do things which result in our lashing out in anger. We are sure that their priorities are all wrong, and we are here to tell them that. Instead, we discover that, in separating ourselves from another, we create our own suffering. It is we who experience pain, even though we are sure our initial intent is to inflict it upon them. The contrast between the suffering we feel and the loving space we were in before our anger is so great, we realize that the only way we will be able to return to our own peace is to mend this sense of separation. Sometimes we do this sooner rather than later and sometimes we never do it, and hence we suffer in our own sense of separation for a lifetime. This is why all forgiveness is self-forgiveness.

Believe it or not, we are all doing the best we can do. In accepting that, we can forgive all others anything, and we do it for our own sake. As soon as we speak some words of forgiveness toward the other, we are released from our own discomfort. We begin to see that we are always responsible for our own state of being. We can make ourselves happy and peaceful or we can choose to be miserable. It is important to express the anger when it arises, to release it from our bodies (and indeed to express our own truth as we see it to remain in integrity with ourselves), but it is equally important to make amends so that we can return to peace and love. My peaceful and loving state is more important to me than all the supposed lessons I think I'm going to teach someone else.

In the awareness of all that I have learned, I choose peace instead of pain. I choose love instead of anger. I choose oneness instead of separation. I choose radiant life, and all is well.

Affirmation:

I rest in the peace of my own creation! I choose love over pain and suffering. I behold the presence of God within me!

The Finisher of your Faith

As you passionately devote yourself to knowing God, you will be able to override the demands of the little ego and faithfully surrender to the One who is the finisher of your faith.

Michael Bernard Beckwith, *Forty-Day Mind Fast Soul Feast*

Surrender is not about giving up; it's about giving in to your soul's calling. God is indeed the finisher of the divine project known as you. Your faith in a love intelligence which is greater than yourself, by whatever name you choose to call it, propels you in the direction of your freedom and greatness.

As you move along on the spiritual path, you begin to witness events in your life which reinforce your faith. As your faith is reinforced, you feel safe enough to surrender a little more, and so it continues. Finally, you begin to see that your security lies within you and not in the external accumulation of material goods. You begin to see that the love you seek outside yourself is who and what you already are. You begin to see that your belief in your own poor health has kept you from experiencing the vital, energetic and healthy body that God created, calling it you. You begin to see that the wisdom of the ages lives within you—speaking to you, guiding and directing you. You begin to see that there is nothing to get in the world—only a world to be experienced in every present moment of your life—only eyes to be looked into, and love to be shared and a whole new world to be experienced from the perspective of the awakened one. Then you desire to fill your senses more and more with the beauty and light that is available to those who have the eyes to see and the ears to hear.

Yes, God is the finisher of your faith. Great things are in store for one who surrenders. Don't be afraid to let go. Your divine life depends upon it!

Affirmation:

I am willing to surrender into my own infinite possibility! I am a beloved creation of the Divine! I rejoice in my new-found freedom as an awakened one!

The World of your Creation

We are yet to become aware... that we embrace our world within ourselves; that all that exists as persons, places and things lives only within our own consciousness. We could never become aware of anything outside the realm of our own mind.

Joel Goldsmith, *The Infinite Way*

We have heard the phrase, "Nothing is happening outside of yourself." The words of Joel Goldsmith enable me to see even more clearly that my whole world is within my consciousness. In other words, everything I see and experience is interpreted by and perceived through my consciousness. Each of us interprets and perceives the world differently based on our individual consciousness. My spiritual work carries me higher and higher in consciousness until I'm living more and more in the absolute truth of God as my very life. The God Presence then within me is the only reality, and it is absolute for where is there to go beyond the infinite nature of God?

If the world you are seeing is not to your liking, that is a call to do your spiritual work. Your life is a matter of perception and you can change your perception. There are no victims. This is a concept which is very difficult to accept and understand, particularly from a limited awareness of consciousness. To the degree you hold yourself in this belief of your victimhood, or anyone else's, that is where you remain stuck.

Ultimately, nothing holds you in bondage but your own limited thinking. As you begin the quest to truly know yourself, you move into the flow and your life expresses more peace, love, joy and harmony—it becomes a celebration of the only life there is, which is God at the very center of your being! It has nothing to do with any person or circumstance outside of yourself; it flows from the grace within you! With God at the center of your being, all things are possible!

Affirmation:

I let myself be free in God! I open myself to the wonders of the universe! I release myself from limited thinking! I am born again in Spirit!

Me and My Shadow

To own one's own shadow is to reach a holy place—an inner center—not attainable in any other way. To fail this is to fail one's own sainthood and to miss the purpose of life.

Robert A. Johnson, *Owning Your Own Shadow*

There are things about all of us that we are ashamed of, or disgusted by—things that we repress and lock away within ourselves as we go about making what we think of as a better life. They might be the things about us that we've struggled to overcome and that we'd just as soon forget. Or feelings we have that we don't want to face. Or anger or hurt that has not been dealt with. Or fear about something that we avoid. Whatever is there lays in wait for the innocent ones on whom we project it. All the violence, racial hatred, and wars stem from the outer projection of individuals who have not done their inner shadow work.

Doing your shadow work allows the loving to expand within you. It sets you free from needing to judge others because they are different from you. It is seeing innocence where you once placed fear; it is feeling love where you once chose disgust; it is accepting what may never change, and being at peace with what is. It is seeing beyond appearances to witness God in the flesh.

Where there is willingness to become clear and clean, we are grateful to know our spiritual work will take us deep into our own shadow side. No stone is left unturned as we say yes to God. In owning, accepting and loving our own shadow, we are made whole and holy, and we become an instrument through which the world is healed.

Affirmation:

I gratefully embrace my shadow side and call it holy! I radiate loving acceptance of all that is! I willingly let go of all my fear and doubt! I fully embrace all that I am as God's perfect creation!

Defenseless

Let them ever shout for joy, because thou defendest them…

Holy Bible, Psalm 5:11

Through spiritual discernment, we see that we have within us a power which is greater than anything we shall ever contact…

Ernest Holmes, *The Science of Mind*

As I am fully aware of myself and who I am, there is nothing for me to defend against. There is nothing that I need to win for I have already won. It is a surrendered state, but powerful beyond measure. I am surrendered to that within me which is pure integrity, pure love and pure wisdom. I have nothing to prove for I am the proof.

The need to defend is ego-based. All the mind chatter that says we have something to prove or some position to defend comes from a disbelief in the perfection within us. Life becomes simple when we no longer have to prove anything to the world outside of ourselves. When we focus instead on self-mastery and our own personal spiritual evolution, we are set free to soar to the heights of our own being. From that way of being, the world then becomes our cheerleader. To the degree that we do not experience the world as our cheerleader, we are still caught in ego gratification. Therein lies our work.

How good it is to be free from performing for someone else's approval! I constantly go within and ask if what is before me is for my highest good. I find myself wanting to provide what my soul is seeking in every moment. It does not appear as a self-absorbed, selfish life because my soul only desires to love and serve and experience beauty of all kinds. I am grateful to know that I am my supply and the universe is devoted to my well-being.

Affirmation:

I am defenseless, for I am Pure Spirit. My way is made smooth before me. I live with my eye turned inward. I am that which I seek.

The Practice of Being Ordinary

Gandhi wrote, "I claim to be no more than an average person with less than average ability... Any man or woman can achieve what I have if he or she would make the same effort and cultivate the same hope and faith."

Wayne Muller, *Legacy of the Heart*

Muller continues in his book, "Gandhi placed no more value on his own life than he did on the parents who gave him birth and raised him, on the farmers who grew the food that fed him, or on his followers who did so much of the work."

The idea that we are more special than the rest keeps us in separation. Tibetan Monk Tara Rinpoche has said, "The intensity of our sorrow will vary in direct proportion to the intensity of our feeling that 'I am important'." The truth is we are all special and truly capable of great things.

What I realized with this new awareness is that I am now free to connect and give my love without regard for what I'm getting back. As Tara Rinpoche says, the degree to which you need to see yourself as important in other people's eyes is the degree to which you will suffer.

We were born in perfection. We are supported by a Love Intelligence that delights in its creation called you. In your ordinariness, you are beyond comparison. There is nothing you have to prove in order to be loved. God loves you beyond anything you can imagine because you are its divine creation.

Affirmation:

I am a perfect child of the earth! God's love pours forth into me lighting up my life! I am free to give all I have to give!

Heaven on Earth

When the time comes that nothing goes forth from you other than that which you would be glad to have return, then you will have reached your heaven.

Ernest Holmes, *This Thing Called You*

To live from a place of good intention is not often easy. What do you do with all your negative thoughts and opinions? Being human, we do have them, and they take us out of our own peace and love inside.

As we become more keenly aware of who we truly are, a part of us acts as observer, monitoring our thoughts, words, and deeds. We see that everything we think, say, and do is a choice. We see that we are always at choice about whether we experience heaven or hell. To stay in peace and love inside is to experience heaven on earth.

Look for what is good in a situation, or see how you can reframe it in your mind, to return to the peace and love that you are. Sometimes this is difficult because our own buttons are pushed. We are confronted by one of our own issues, and we would instead like to engage in our righteousness. I've done it both ways. Ultimately, I feel better when I do what it takes to stay centered in God. Gossip and negative activity simply do not provide what I'm ultimately looking for—peace and love.

When I stay in the loving, love returns to me multiplied. When I stay in the peace, I am fortified in Spirit. Stay in the loving, and all your desires are fulfilled. God is your life! The richness of just knowing that is enough to sustain you through anything. You stand in a freedom and power that is unsurpassed. Be on the side of love in all things, and you will have reached heaven on earth!

Affirmation:

I radiate only love wherever I am! I set my intention to experience heaven on earth! I am supported by a benevolent universe! I am an emissary of the divine.

True Nobility

There is no nobility in being superior to some other person...
True nobility is being superior to your previous self.

Hindu Proverb

True nobility is freedom from comparing yourself to another. God does not compare. God holds you in a love so profound, it is beyond any human experience of love.

True nobility is surrendering to that within you which knows its supreme connection to God. True nobility is holding yourself to the highest standard of your God self, not some standard contrived by someone or something outside of yourself. True nobility means that sometimes you stand alone humanly. However, you are never truly alone, for the experience of God in your life is constant and unchanging. True nobility is living in love, peace, and forgiveness with the courage of a warrior. It takes great courage to face your fear and do the work necessary to return to peace and love inside.

True nobility offers the gift of great freedom. True nobility does not show up as weakness, but rather boldly as great power. One stands defenseless, but with the kind of clarity that can reach all manner of men and women—for the truth shines forth like a light in the darkness.

God loves you uncompromisingly just as you are! You do not need to fix anything, just recognize yourself as God sees you. Therein you stand in true nobility!

Affirmation:

I let go of any desire to compare myself to another. I accept myself fully as a radiant creation of the divine. I am unsurpassed in my perfection as I stand in true nobility!

Sublime Existence

The soul cannot fully express itself unless physical existence is all that it can be on the physical plane, and the body is not fully alive until the soul is awakened on the spiritual plane.

Christian D. Larson, *The Pathway of Roses*

Oftentimes I have heard people deny some aspect of life on the physical plane in their pursuit of a life of excellence on the religious or spiritual level. It's as though they believe that God does not reside in all that is physical. If that were true, why would we have these bodies, and why would we have our amazing ability to see, hear, touch, taste, and feel? Why would there be such a myriad and variety of wonderful things to look at? Why would there be so many different smells to smell, tastes to taste, surfaces to feel and sound to hear? Why would we be here in this physical experience?

There is a purpose to this physical expression. We are here to create; and as we awaken on the soul level, what we create and contribute is so wonderful and needed on the planet. We are indeed then doing God's work, and God's work is to love and be loved.

Sometimes it is hard to integrate all that we know about life on the physical and soul levels. I like to think, as Christian D. Larson so beautifully states, that we are physical beings living in an infinite spiritual sea. We are here to embrace every aspect of our being, knowing that it is all God in its radiance! As we awaken on the soul level, there is only greater joy and beauty that we see on the physical level. We are meant to live in that perfect joy, beauty and love. We are not meant to be deprived of anything worthy in the physical expression. We are here to have it all!

Affirmation:

I gratefully embrace my wonderful body and the infinite nature of my soul! I have everything I need to live a glorious life! My cup truly runneth over!

How Deep Is Your Love?

An authentically empowered person lives in love. Love is the energy of the soul. Love is what heals the personality. There is nothing that cannot be healed by love. There is nothing but love.

Gary Zukav, *The Seat of the Soul*

The love you experience with another is within you. When you love deeply and the other person leaves for whatever reason, through death or choice, you have not lost the love. That love is your own, which you have allowed to be accessed through the blessing of another one in your life. This is very good news for those who attach the love known to the one they knew it with. If you say, "There will never be another love like the one I had with (fill in the blank)," you are making a choice not to experience your own love at that level again. The truth is, the love within you is infinite and will go as deep as you allow it to go as often as you allow it to go there.

Humanly, we are constantly making choices about our willingness to love. We are deciding how much and how often. If you feel that there is not enough love in your life, then choose to love more deeply more often and more freely. There is enough love in you for several lifetimes!

I ask myself today, what can I do to experience the love within me more deeply? How can I give more love today? As I let myself experience the deep love within me, it is exquisite. There is nothing that surpasses it. I experience the thrill of love, pure love, and oneness toward whomever I am with. In that, I have joined God and I feel exhilarated. I think only love and I am there!

Affirmation:

I bask in the radiant presence of my own loving! I transcend all appearances! I give and receive love abundantly!

Oneness

Then said the Lord to him, put off thy shoes from thy feet: for the place where thou standest is holy ground.

Holy Bible, Acts 7:33

Thou will keep him in perfect peace, whose mind is stayed on thee...

Holy Bible, Isaiah 26:3

Perhaps the most elusive of all the spiritual concepts is the idea that we are all one. Now, more than ever, we must anchor that truth in our consciousness for the transformation of our planet.

It is important that, even in recognizing ourselves as spiritual beings, we do not separate ourselves from those who we believe have not yet come to an understanding of their true identity as divine beings. We do not want to wage a war in our righteousness against anyone, even those we think live in ignorance. Instead, we stand firm in the midst of seeming chaos on the planet, remembering that we must individually be what we wish to experience.

We are one with all life—no matter what it looks like. At times like these, it is so hard to accept and embody that truth; but only in embodying that truth will the world survive and pull itself out of the darkness into the light. We are one with a terrorist who would fly a plane into a building full of people. We are one with the politician who would make every decision based on his or her own personal gain. We are one with bombers, murderers and thieves.

It is easy to talk spiritual principles, but in times like these, it is imperative that each of us begin to live these principles in such a way that when you see me, you see the God that created me. Our charge now is to hold the light for those who cannot see it, to stand centered in our divine identity, and to not waver in our love of God and all mankind!

Affirmation:

I live what I wish to experience! I stand firm in the purity of my love! I am an instrument of God's peace!

The Divine Instrument

It is the Spirit of God which can find outlet only as human consciousness, as your consciousness and mine.

Joel Goldsmith, *Practicing the Presence*

As we deepen in the realization of our true identity as a divine emanation of God, we become increasingly available. We become witness to the beauty all around us; and somehow in our witnessing of that beauty, it is enhanced in, and appreciated by others who come into our presence. Suddenly, in our surrender to this greater authority within us, we see more clearly now, and our clarity diminishes the world's confusion.

Letting go of our own harm and unforgiveness provides an avenue for others to do the same. We know that we are sourced by the Holy Spirit, and we let go of our fear. God moves in, through, and as us, and we bask in grace—a grace that comforts and extends its peace everywhere we are. There is a sense of God's delight as its high vibration of love can flow freely now, through us, without restriction, extending itself out into all manner of physical expression. Oh yes, God is rejoicing now, and the joy within me is magnified! All my needs are met in this divine, eternal dance. I am sourced, and I am sourcing.

Suddenly, it doesn't seem to matter what I do for a living or where I am standing geographically, because everywhere I am is heaven on earth! Where there is war, I am peace. Where there is pain and suffering, I am comfort and solace. Where there is weakness, I am strength. Where there is unhappiness, I am joy. Where there is hatred, I am love.

I am so grateful to be an instrument of the Divine. I see that if God be for me, no thing can be against me, and I am truly blessed—this day and eternally.

Affirmation:

I willingly release any resistance to my good! I allow myself to be in the eternal flow of the universe! I bask in the pure and radiant love of God!

Moments of My High Resolve

Keep Fresh before me the moments of my high resolve, that......
in good times or in tempests, in the days when the darkness
and the foe are nameless or unfamiliar, I may not forget that to
which my life is committed.

Howard Thurman, *For the Inward Journey*

May I remain in faith when horrible catastrophe strikes. May I see truth when human appearance causes me confusion. May I stay in my loving when hate is coming at me. May I see God before me in the most hate-filled person. May I be able to see goodness as it arises out of pain. May I forgive even what I think is unforgivable.

May I surrender when I want to fight. May I feel my freedom when I'm imprisoned—either physically or by my thoughts. May I keep rising out of the ashes of despair and not falter. May I shine my light in utter darkness. May I have a vision when my dreams appear to be crumbling. May I be fully present when I want to disappear. May I stand in my integrity when it would be easier to sacrifice it. May I speak my truth when I would choose to keep quiet.

May I be a place of refuge in an otherwise fearful and violent world. May I love my neighbor when I would rather judge him. May I surrender my anger and irritation in the name of my own peace.

May I remember to pray when I am lost. May I see and feel the joy in all that is joyful. May I play and dance and sing, and not hold back for fear of seeming foolish.

May I accept all aspects of my being and see them as holy. May I see myself as God in the flesh and stay humbled. May I soar to the heights of my own being when it's more comfortable to stay small. May the love within me cancel out everything unlovable so that I am peaceful in thy love.

O Spirit, I am willing to accept thy will and thy goodness as my life.

Affirmation:

I keep fresh before me the moments of my high resolve. I remember that to which my life is committed. I am inseparable from my source.

Seek First God's Kingdom

When we enter the spiritual life we gain every quality...(to make) life full and complete in our own... being; and we gain the power to produce and create in the external world whatever we may need or desire.

Christian D. Larson, *The Pathway of Roses*

Sometimes I forget what I know, and I begin to focus on what I perceive as a problem in my life in order to come up with some remedy for fixing it. The minute I move into that place of focusing my intention on the supposed problem, I begin a downward spiral, which lasts as long as my forgetfulness about spiritual truth. We often hear that you cannot fix the problem at the level of the problem, but we all forget because we are human beings used to doing and problem solving.

The words from Christian D. Larson remind me that the answers to all my problems lie in my willingness to know more of God as me and to stay focused on that. If I focus on meditation, prayer and my oneness with all that is, I am delivered out of the darkness into the light; I am delivered out of fear into certain knowing that if God be for me, no thing can be against me. Therein lies my salvation, for I recognize that I am a spiritual being. In my awareness of that truth, all things are possible, and I am released from the bondage of fear and doubt. Absolute freedom is gained as one adverse condition after another disappears.

What we learn as our consciousness is raised is that the power within us can create and produce all of our desires and can do so with ease and grace. We see that we have the power of choice and, as we begin to choose only that which is life-promoting, we see that all our needs are met in God.

Turning within to the presence of God soothes and comforts me. As I place God first in my life, all things are added unto me.

Affirmation:

I seek God first! In that I am released from all fear and doubt! All my needs are met with grace and ease!

Believers

The Spirit of Christ... constructively uses the law. The Spirit of the AntiChrist is the destructive use of the law. The Spirit of Christ... will always transcend, neutralize, destroy and utterly obliterate the Spirit of the Antichrist.

Ernest Holmes, *The Science of Mind*

The world is being rescued by the believers—the ones who do not fear death. They are the ones who live in love and who practice the principles of oneness and inclusivity. The believers see the light and the new world. They see beyond appearances and beyond materialism. The believers know that if you prepare for war, you will have war; and they know that if you prepare for peace, you will have peace.

The believers are rising now in the midst of chaos to remind us of God's love. The believers are forming a grid across the planet. They are unified in the truth of human existence—that God is real and lives within each one of us. There is no power greater than the love of God. The believers know that evil is not a thing in and of itself; it is merely a misuse of the law of freedom.

I am witness now to the transformation on the planet. My vision, which is far-reaching is one of peace, joy, love, freedom, abundance and grace. I will not be pulled from my vision through fear because I know the power of love, and there is no greater power on the planet. I see a world being transformed through the love of God. This power, this presence, is enough to restore sanity to a seemingly insane, out-of-control world. There is a groundswell of goodness, truth, generosity, and loving upon the planet. This I see and welcome now. My vision is a great one, for God is great! I rest in the power of love.

Affirmation:

I release all fear thoughts right now! I rest in the absolute assurance of God's love! I am perfect peace, perfect love, and perfect being!

To Serve One Master

I know that the realization of Life and Love within me heals all who come into its presence. I silently bless all who enter my atmosphere. It is not I, but the Father who dwelleth in me, He doeth the works.

Ernest Holmes, *The Science of Mind*

I see that my entire life is one of service. Everywhere I am, I serve my one and only master—the Self of me, which is not separate from God. I am sure that I am not even always aware of the ways in which I have served God, but I know that I am God's obedient servant. I have received internal direction or guidance that I have obeyed, even when my human mind might have called it imprudent; however, I am always clear when it is a call from On High. When I receive that call, I know that I have been blessed, and there is no other action to take but one of absolute surrender and compliance. Every time I serve from that space, I am rewarded tenfold, and it is in the service itself that I receive an enormous gift of love beyond compare. I do not serve when I am not in integrity to do so, and I constantly look inside to see if I am in integrity with Self (God) and that I am truly serving God by my action, and not my own ego.

I see that we live in an abundant universe. There is always enough time, money and love to share—one way or the other. The more you think that is not so, the less you have to give; and at that point, it is time to reevaluate whether you are serving God or your own ego. One must nurture the Self (God), love the Self (God) in order to be a place of love, giving and true service.

God so loves and cherishes its beloved. As we stay tuned in to that Indwelling Presence, that is the place that meets love, beauty, grace and goodness everywhere it is and the place from which the greatest service is given as it shines its light everywhere it is.

Affirmation:

I am God's obedient servant! I am tuned in to divine direction! I live from the inside out!

Arise!

Negation… can never be an ultimate truth. Life cannot operate against itself. Always the negative is overcome by the positive. Good cannot fail to overcome evil. The meek alone shall inherit the earth.

Ernest Holmes, *This Thing Called You*

As I reflect on my life, I see that all the events (many of which I deemed quite negative at the time) have brought me to the awareness of this unique expression that I am today. For that, I am eternally grateful and have no regrets. The ultimate truth of my life is that the part of me that is eternal life has never been touched by hurt or betrayal, for it lives in the illumination of Divine Spirit.

I lost my way for a time, confused by the human circumstances of my life; but ultimately, I came to realize that the unique something inside of me, the Divine Presence within me—my essential self—would never die or be damaged in any way from its perfection. Once I came to that realization, I could see that I would no longer be at the effect of the outer world. I could choose instead to live from the inside out. Therein lies the transforming power of each individual to create a new world and a new experience. Good does prevail over evil, because darkness is unconscious!

We awaken to the truth of our being. We are perfection itself! We do not get caught up in mind chatter that has nothing to do with the truth of who we are. We tap into universal intelligence and allow ourselves to be divinely guided to our bliss. We see that we were never separate from all that is holy and divine. We are sheltered by the presence of Spirit and its love for us. We step into a new way of being in the world where we focus on what we want—not on what we don't want. We focus on beauty, love, peace, freedom, light, grace, abundance and truth. We focus our attention on God and release our fearful thinking. Yes, this is a new day for a new you as you arise in your greater glory!

Affirmation:

I arise in God! I embrace all that I am as Divine Spirit! I am set free to soar to the heights of my being! I am willing to be great!

The Realized Presence Within You

In your heart, dwell upon the gift which has been given you, delivered to you from the Father—the gift of the realized Presence within you. Bless it always that it may increase.

Joel S. Goldsmith, *Practicing the Presence*

You have come to have life and have it more abundantly. You have come to create heaven on earth. Your little mind will not serve you in this, for indeed you are creating in the realm of the infinite.

To embrace all that we are as Spirit, we must move past finite thinking into the realm of infinite possibility. We must be willing to step over the precipice of the unknown in faith and trust. We must be willing to surrender our need to control every activity of our lives. We must be willing to release the unforgiveness that has found sanctuary inside of us.

We must be willing to both give and receive love; each is equally important in the cycle of life. We must be willing to surrender our need to be right, and choose peace and harmony instead. We must be willing to expose and extricate our internal demons, relinquishing them into the Light. We must be willing to stand out from the crowd. We must be willing to say "Yes!" to that higher authority within us, even when it seems imprudent to do so from the perspective of our little human self.

Everything that has ever happened to you brings you ultimately to perfect self-realization. Embrace all of your life as necessary for your divine fulfillment. God's creation is dynamic, whole and complete. You are made in the image and likeness of that which created you out of Itself and called it good. Do not settle for less than the magnificence you were born to be.

The love God has for you surpasses any idea you have ever had about love. Awaken now to the Realized Presence within you.

Affirmation:

I awaken now to my God Self! I see clearly as never before!

Surrender

The Lord is my shepherd; I shall not want.

Holy Bible, Psalm 23:1

Negativity, unhappiness or suffering—in whatever form—means that there is resistance and resistance is always unconscious.

Eckhart Tolle, *The Power of Now*

When we speak of surrender from a spiritual framework, we are talking about whether or not we are willing to be in the dynamic flow of the universe. The dynamic flow is easy and it is effortless. The only other choice is resistance. As Eckhart Tolle tells us, all negativity, unhappiness and suffering come from resistance. Resistance is arguing with what is. There are things that will not and cannot change no matter how much we argue with ourselves over them. In our acceptance is our freedom.

Surrender does not mean powerlessness. Surrender, as I'm speaking of it, simply means acceptance of what is. As you move in the dynamic flow of the universe, there are still plenty of opportunities for choice but life becomes very real and uncomplicated. We create the complexities of life with all of our egoic mind chatter. The ego fears its vulnerability. Yet, as we are reminded in *The Power of Now,* "It is only through the letting go of resistance, through becoming vulnerable, that we can discover our true and essential invulnerability." Therein lies our greatest power!

As we continue in our spiritual growth and unfoldment, the pain we experience is fear-based resistance to the unknown life that awaits us. For the true Self to be revealed, some aspect of us is continually dying. We must have the courage to step through our fear into our own greater glory. We are fulfilling God's promise as we emerge in the fullness of who we are as Divine Beings.

Do not fear! God never deserts us for It loves us beyond our own limited understanding of love! Step forward now in celebration of your Divine Self!

Affirmation:

I willingly release all resistance to what is! I surrender my life into the dynamic flow of the universe! I allow the love of God to be my source and supply!

The Joy of Being

Those who have not found their true wealth, which is the radiant joy of Being and the deep, unshakable peace that comes with it, are beggars even if they have great material wealth.

Eckhart Tolle, *The Power of Now*

I accept myself as the Beloved. Figuratively, I have knelt at the feet of the Master Teacher. I have seen my own transgressions and conversely, have witnessed my own perfection. I am assured in this moment of God's love for me and with that love, fear dissipates. I stand unarmored for I see now that I need no weapons or defenses.

This expanded love within is all I need. I leave all worry and doubt behind, for it does not serve me and has no place in this new awareness of my being. I am alight with the fire of God. I need not proclaim it from the rooftops; it is the very breath I take and the walk I walk. I surrender now all the false perceptions that have allowed me to doubt myself.

In witnessing the truth of my life and God's unconditional love, I can rest in peace. The agitation within me diminishes. This holy gift blesses me and enables me to let go of the mind chatter, which often times contradicts my true nature as a spiritual being.

In this restful state, I am able to see that my human doing sometimes interferes with my human being. There is comfort now as I simply rest in what I know. My source and supply are endless. I am provided with all I need. My life is answered prayer and a testimony of God's love. I am committed now to my own self-acceptance. I accept myself exactly as I am, and I love myself as God loves me.

Affirmation:

God's infinite love blazes within me! I am a creation of the Divine!

The Extraordinary in the Ordinary

God has a gift to give to the world as you, beyond what your surface mentality may sometimes see.

Michael Bernard Beckwith, *Forty Day Mind Fast Soul Feast*

There is nothing that is ordinary, for truly God created everything out of itself and called it good. It is our human ego that puts names on things and calls them good or bad, less or more. It is our human ego that allows us to devalue a simple servant or homeless person and place a prince, king or politician on a pedestal. Truly, God blesses and loves us all. God does not play favorites. There is no greater or lesser in God so if you look at your life and say, "I am not worthy because I have not done great things," the truth is that you can do great things no matter what you do for a living.

You have great value and worth to God, no matter what your accomplishments. The fact is, right where you are now, you can affect and change lives for the better. Begin with your own life. The way to begin is to recognize that you are a spiritual being created in the image and likeness of God. The depth of God's love for you has no bounds. You are so loved, beyond any human idea of love. Once you begin to realize and embrace the idea of God's love for you, you cannot help but become a messenger of the light for it is the light within you that enables others to see, sense and know the light within themselves.

You were born into greatness as a spiritual being. Step into your extraordinariness now. Begin to serve the Indwelling Presence within you. It is God, and God is great. Be willing to be great for God.

Affirmation:

I am extraordinary for I am a divine creation! I let go of my little life and allow God to express through me.

A New Reality

We have thought that outside things controlled us, when all the time we have had that within which could have changed everything and given us freedom from bondage.

Ernest Holmes, *The Science of Mind*

A friend of mine was complaining that she had once again been betrayed by her husband through his infidelity. He had been unfaithful early in their marriage, but it was never dealt with.... just swept under the rug. I asked her if she has ever trusted him since the first time she learned of his unfaithfulness. She said no, she hasn't. I realized in that instant that, in addition to his betraying her, she had also betrayed herself. Something within her did not trust him and she chose to ignore it. This is the way in which we create our experience—either consciously or unconsciously—and upon realization, this is the way we can begin to step out of our victimhood.

In what ways are you betraying yourself? What do you know about your life but are refusing to face? It is important to take responsibility for what goes on in your life. Things don't "just happen" to us. We often set ourselves up for the very thing we fear the most. Perhaps some of us do not want to be personally responsible. Maybe we want to blame other people for our misery, but the conscious, awakened one cannot do that.

The conscious, awakened one delights in the idea of having the personal power to create heaven on earth. The conscious, awakened one sees the benefit of creating from awareness and enlightenment. The conscious, awakened one is willing to take personal responsibility for the experiences in his or her life.

Being asleep is painful. Being awake is to come alive to the infinite possibility of your life. Being awake is to live in joy and peace and harmony and abundance. Being awake is to walk in prayer and love. Oh yes, being awake is so much easier than walking asleep. In the waking up, we can take dominion over our lives and truly begin to experience heaven on earth.

Affirmation:

I wake up to the glory of God as me! I willingly take personal responsibility for my life! I freely release my victimhood! I claim my life as a conscious creator!

Reflections on Love

Through your loving, existence and nonexistence merge. All opposites unite. All that is profane becomes sacred again.

Rumi

I am a lover. My job is to stay in my loving, no matter what comes into my experience.

The challenge in relationship is always my willingness to make a choice for love. We often want the other person to think as we think, do as we do and, more or less, to be just like us. We judge and attack this person we call our beloved, in an effort to hold on. We want to possess him or her (as if that were possible), and our fear of abandonment runs us.

Fortunately, another way of being in the world exists which allows everyone around us to thrive. When we are so filled with Love inside—love of God, love of self, all the same—feeling loved is not dependent upon what we receive from outside of ourselves. It is dependent upon what we know of Love itself—that it is in inexhaustible supply and is the very name and nature of each of us as a God-being.

When you know that kind of love for yourself, you are set free from your attachment to having things your own way, from your need to judge and possess another, and from your fear of abandonment. And, miraculously, everyone else in your presence is set free too.

Love is God's eternal promise to us. The love within me expands; I cannot turn it on and off. It is the fullness of me. It does not give of itself in a qualified way; it simply is.

I am a lover. My job is simply to stay in my loving no matter what comes into my experience.

Affirmation:

I choose love! I willingly let go and allow the fullness of God to express as me! I stand in my harmlessness everywhere I am! I joyfully make a choice for love!

To Live Each Season

*So live each season as it passes; breathe the air, drink the drink,
taste the fruit, and resign yourself to the influences of each.*

Henry David Thoreau, *Journal Entry for August 23, 1853*

I prayed for a shift in perception because I could not see another
way. I did not even realize how locked in I was to thinking that
certain aspects of my life had to remain in place in order for me to
survive well. I had not embodied the idea that God is my source,
even though I said it a million times. So I took a baby step in prayer,
because I could not take a big one in physical action. Now I can see
where I am the only limiting force in my life—a great discovery for
a seeker of truth!

The truth is, each of us is perfectly free and can have it all. There is
no limit to what God has in store for us. Our work is always to see
where we are blocking our own good, because the universe is never
blocking it. Thinking makes it so.

What are you thinking? Are you thinking about how it feels to have
the very thing you are craving, or are you thinking about the reasons
you don't have it? Are you thinking about the unlimited possibility
of your life, or are you thinking about being limited in some way? Do
you believe that you have to be in a certain place, even if you don't

like it, in order to be safe? If you don't know how to get unstuck, then pray for a change in perception. Prayer is always answered because God never deserts its beloved.

We are imprisoned by our own limited thinking. How willing are you to be set free of your own imprisonment? Set yourself free to live each day with the acceptance, enthusiasm and joy of a child. The little children shall lead them!

Affirmation:

I am willing to change my perception! I see now that there are a million paths to freedom. I release all limitations I placed on God's idea for my life! I am set free to live my dreams!

Live for Now

*Surrender is the simple but profound wisdom of yielding to...
the flow of life. The only place where you can experience the
flow of life is in the Now, so to surrender is to accept the present
moment unconditionally and without reservation.*

Eckhart Tolle, *The Power of Now*

Do you understand that you are never done? You never get it done!
So rest and enjoy the journey. That, more than any other awareness,
will bring you back to living each precious moment in the Now.
There is no end goal, so breathe and relax. Take a look around you
and really see where you are and whom you are with. What are you
waiting for? It is here now. You are a living theology. Sometimes we
become as goal-oriented about our spiritual work as we are about
our jobs or other areas of our lives, but the time to smell the roses
is right now.

We spend so much of our time either regretting the past or preparing
for the future. We are imprisoned by our own faulty thinking. The
past is no more; it is over. Today is a brand new day that truly has
nothing to do with the past in terms of how you choose to live your
life right now. And the future either may never come or won't come
in the way you've planned, so give it up and start living today. It is
just a choice away. It is so much easier to live for Now, to take care

of the business at hand today, to be fully present in each moment. What a gift you then bring to the world and to yourself.

There is nothing more wonderful than to be seen and heard or to really see and hear another. All the pressure is off and what remains is devotion to the moment at hand. You are then truly God's precious servant in every breath you take; so right now, stop, breathe and love.

Affirmation:

God is my life! I am filled with delight! I shall not be moved from my devotion! I am richly blessed and a rich blessing!

Your Glorious Life Awaits Your Realization

For thou art my rock and my fortress; therefore for thy name's sake lead me and guide me.

Holy Bible, Psalm 31:3

Sometimes we are so heavy laden, we cannot imagine how we will ever get out of our feelings of despair and hopelessness. We have told our stories of woe so many times, we have become the story; and even though the "events" happened so long ago, we live them over and over again, suffering all the while. Your story has become what defines you, but you truly are not your story.

There is a way out of the darkness into the light of a new day. It is within your power to change your life if you are willing. Nothing is insurmountable for one who loves God. God will never give up on you for you are a creation of God just as surely as are the trees, flowers, sun and moon. You were born in perfection and wholeness. The question is: How do you realize that about yourself when you are caught up in the web of your own self-abuse? How do you begin to see that you are divine because you are Infinite Spirit? How do you see and appreciate that you are living in a unified field of awareness that is always for you and never against you—that you are "the Thing Itself" and that there is infinite power within you?

If you truly desire to break free from your story, then begin by setting an intention to do so. Begin to pray every day to see yourself as God sees you. State to yourself daily that you are willing to accept and love yourself as God loves you. Find time in the morning and at night to sit in the stillness. It is in the stillness that a deep, profound relationship with God is established. God is awaiting you there. Love begins to expand within the body temple, and a love affair with the Self takes birth unlike any human love ever known.

Great things are awaiting the one who loves God! A great and glorious life is waiting its revelation! Set yourself free from your own imprisonment! God has great things in store for you!

Affirmation:

I willingly surrender my life to God! I eagerly let go of my negative story and refuse to let it run my life! I am set free now to live the glorious life God has in store for me!

Self-Reliance

Nothing can bring you peace but yourself. Nothing can bring you peace but the triumph of principles.

Ralph Waldo Emerson, *Self-Reliance*

Whenever we look outside ourselves for a circumstance that we believe will bring us great peace inside, we are heading in the direction of attachment to an outcome. In that attachment, we can lose sight of our oneness with God and create the very duality we wish to avoid. At that moment, we move from evolved spiritual consciousness to the personality level...and our personal anger, pain and suffering begin.

We cannot exit this suffering as long as we remain in the domain of right and wrong. When we are able to do our prayer work from higher ground, and to stay focused on the unified consciousness—the unified field of awareness—we can see that the person or situation we might label as our enemy is actually our own self.

Emerson's "triumph of principles" refers to what each of us experiences when we stay in absolute alignment with the principles we espouse as practitioners of Truth. This is a great charge presented to us, because it is so much easier to take a stand—even a righteous one—and operate from the personality level. (We probably have had more practice with that.)

What God desires of us, though, is to stand in the love that is inherent in our nature—a love so powerful that it is transformative. We cannot know the ways in which prayer and love create. If we try to figure it out and create some outcome from the personality level, it never rises to the level of greatness that God has in store for us... nor will it last as long.

So let us claim our divine power and stand in the absolute truth of our existence. As we pray from the exalted essence of our being, we are able to behold the miracles of God's creation. Prayer is always answered!

Affirmation:

I remember who I am! I stand resolute in the love of God! I am a place of peace and love on the planet!

Perfection As You

It is by love that we approach God.

Aimee Martin

The best and most beautiful things in the world cannot be seen or even touched—they must be felt with the heart.

Helen Keller

It's never too late to change our minds, for God as us is love. If we are not in love, we are not tuned into the truth of our lives.

As human beings, we are so invested in our ego, our desire to have others see things through our perception, and the need to be right. Give it up! All of that doesn't matter. What matters—the *only* thing that matters—is how much love you are willing to give and how much peace you are willing to have. You were born in greatness, love and peace. Everything you desire comes to you unbidden with ease when you cease the human struggle and concentrate instead on that within you which is pure perfection. If you focus only on the perfection of God, which is you, all things will be added unto you.

Dedicate the next thirty days to accepting expanded consciousness as you, allowing and letting God in as you, and your life will change.

Focus on what you want, not on what you don't want. Watch when your peace is disturbed inside of you, and pray and journal until you return to love. Soon, you will see that any feeling other than peace inside is not welcome.

As you consciously begin to create your life in this way, you will be creating what you want, not what you do not want. You will begin to see the power in the invisible and in yourself; and through this, you will experience true freedom and heaven on earth!

Affirmation:

I live in the peace and love of God! I radiate true acceptance and allow all that I am to come forth! I let the love of God into my life now, and I am resurrected out of the ashes!

The River God

If God is the river, let go of the banks and jump in. Today, do not put your little toe in. That will avail you little. Leap and let go.

Michael Bernard Beckwith

I've been so afraid to leap in. I have been relying on my little human self and what it can do (my job, etc.) to keep me safe all these years, but my little human self can't seem to do enough for me any more. What is bursting forth within me seems to require that I fully embody the reality that God is my source and supply and that Its nature is infinite.

While I am stuck in my fear, though, God is still being God, and soon even the fear, shrouded in God's love, begins to dissipate, for my intention to embody God as my source never waivers. That is how good and vast God's love is: nothing is more powerful; nothing can supersede God's love for one who has the desire and willingness to transcend all limitations and resistance to fully experience it. The River God awaits, delighted with those who finally leap in.

God's love is not greater for the leapers; it's just that they have removed all blocks to experiencing its vastness. They are unencumbered by their own resistance. Can you not see how much energy it takes for the resistance? When energy is no longer spent resisting the one who loves you beyond your own limited idea of love, that energy then is available for divine works!

So, here I stand on the edge, looking over, having no idea what leaping in will avail me in terms of my life path—only knowing that I am being ever so gently nudged closer and closer. The River God is assuring me that I will be safe, that it will take care of my every need, that I need not be afraid. It is inseparable from the Spirit within me which knows no bounds and no fear. My God will not let up on me and my ego until I jump, and I have the feeling that the day I jump will surely be the beginning of my life.

Affirmation:

I leap in the joy of God's love. I let go of my fear, doubt and resistance. I allow the River God to carry me as I stand in perfect alignment with my source and supply.

Spiritual Role Models

It seems to me that it is a matter of spiritual progress when one becomes free not only of the knowledge which is inevitably from the past, but also from the need to know, which is so often permeated by a fear of the unknown and a desire to predict and control...

Ravi Ravindra, *The Quest*

The greater the love expanding within me, the less fear I experience. As the fear is released, the need to control is released. Standing in the mystery of "I don't know" is exciting and often uncomfortable. That is because most of us have had a plan or goal for our education, next job opportunity or place of residence or new relationship. At some point in our spiritual evolution, all that changes and what remains is a vision, accompanied by a willingness to surrender and a willingness to release all attachment to outcomes. I am choosing, in that moment, not to squeeze the vastness of God into my own limited mental categories.

I say yes to that which is in alignment with my inner calling, never knowing where the path is leading. The God within me is the navigator. It is refreshing to march to my own drumbeat, not being too concerned about outer world expectations, letting go more and more of my need to control. I become, in that instant, my own master, a complete servant of God. I am devoted to God. How can I not be, for God is completely loving and giving. Because I know what it feels like to receive it, I desire to realize the fullness of It as me, letting go of any places of separation inside myself. All problems, differences, fear, resistance and confusion melt away in that loving, which is the most powerful force in the world.

So I say to you, God loves you in this way. No human love can match it, so you can cease expecting others to be all things to you. They cannot be. It is for you to be that for yourself. In that, you will set them and yourself free to be all that you can be!

Affirmation:

I rest in the vastness of God's love! I accept myself fully as the love that I am! I joyfully embrace the mystery of life!

The Secret of Creation

The truth that sets you free is that you can experience in imagination what you desire to experience in reality, and by maintaining this experience in imagination, your desire will become an actuality.

Neville, *The Power of Awareness*

I have watched so many of my brothers and sisters desire a thing and yet never seem to get it. Now I can see so clearly that it is because they do not have a mental equivalent of the thing desired, nor do they have the feeling tone of it. Before you can create a desire or condition, you must be able to imagine yourself having it and, further, be able to feel yourself having it. Often the reason you cannot imagine or feel it is because you have some mind chatter going on that resists the very thing you say you want. The universe (God) is constantly giving. You can know with certainty that if you were not resisting somehow, you would have the very thing you desire. Ah, once again, we are left with the responsibility of creating our own experience—good or bad!

The good news here is that you can create an absolutely glorious life because God is constantly giving you the gifts of the Kingdom. God is so good! So, to begin, start imagining the glorious life you desire. Start feeling what each moment of it would feel like. Focus on what you want in your life, rather than on the fact that you don't have it, why you don't have it, why someone else has it and you don't, or who you are blaming because you don't have it, etc., etc., etc.!

God loves you so much and wants you to have all your desires and great joy too! It is all up to you. Will you imagine and feel your way to your greatest glory? Joy awaits you there.

Affirmation:

I imagine my life in God! I let go of mind chatter than keeps me in separation! I create from the infinite possibility that is me!

Thanksgiving—The Divine Doorway

Gratitude is where freedom and destiny meet, because gratitude is a divine doorway to the fulfillment of destiny.

Michael Bernard Beckwith, *40-Day Mind Fast Soul Feast*

Expressing gratitude and thanksgiving for all that delights you is the exact way to create more blessings in your life. In that instant, you have opened yourself up to accept more of God's gifts that are continuously pouring forth upon you. You cannot see them if you are focusing upon what is wrong in your life.

Sometimes we are in such pain and suffering that we cannot see anything good about our lives. I say the fastest way out of your pain and suffering is to look for the positive in all things. Do not argue with what is, but rather search for the good and wondrous all around you. God's creation is everywhere—in the birds, the trees, the flowers, the seasons, the sky, the ocean, the animals, the kindnesses shown, the great memories, the joyful romping of children at play or the innocence of a baby, good food, the love of a friend or soul partner, the miracle of the body and all of its functions—there are so many blessings!

As physical beings, we have said "Yes" to this physical incarnation. We are not here to suffer through it and get out. We are here to romp and play in the vastness of God's splendor! We are here to delight in it, to receive it, to allow it in, to let it inform and guide us. We are truly in heaven on earth if we are willing to open ourselves up to it. God so loves us and desires to give us the Kingdom, but are we willing to receive it?

I am so grateful and thankful for this world of mine. I give great thanks every day for my everyday blessings that grow larger and larger each and every day. I am blessed by my Beloved God to be able to see as God sees.

Affirmation:

I open my eyes to see my blessings! I live my life in gratitude and thanksgiving! I see the miracle of God's creation! I am that miracle!

Breathless Moments

Life is not measured by the number of breaths we take, but by the moments that take our breath away.

George Carlin

Life is to live, not just to exist, yet many of us are just existing. Do you think that is what God has in mind for you—just living in a numbed state, going through daily tasks on automatic pilot, rather bored by your whole existence?

What God gives to us is the vastness of the universe—the potential for a life filled with breathless moments. The possibilities are limitless. What is your true desire? What is it you have wanted to experience but have been afraid to acknowledge even to yourself? The greatest things in life are not known through the intellect; they are experienced in the heart. Allow yourself to feel, to experience, to love, to appreciate all that is in this world of beauty and grace. See this physical world—the creation of God—in all its magnificence and splendor. Open your eyes, open your heart and open up your channels of receiving. The gifts are enormous, and they do take your breath away!

We live in an amazing, complex and giving universe. Become one who is tuned in to seeing and receiving all that is delightful. Allow yourself to bask in the richness of God's infinite creativity. Live in the miracle consciousness and allow yourself to receive the miracles that are waiting to be delivered to you. God is so good, I tell you! Let go of your small thinking and your small, confined little world. The universe is your playground. Do not be afraid to soar. God has created you to soar.

At the end of my life, I want to know that I soared—that my life was well lived and that I fulfilled the desires of my heart. Beloveds, I invite you to say "yes" to life along with me. We cannot fail or make a mistake because God is truly our source and supply.

Affirmation:

I stand in my absolute faith and love of God! I willingly receive the blessings of the universe! I joyfully dance the dance of the Divine!

The Simple Truth—A Call of the Soul

Then said Jesus to those Jews which believed on him, If ye continue in my word, then are ye my disciples indeed; and ye shall know the truth, and the truth shall make you free.

Holy Bible, St. John 8:31,32

Sometimes we are caught up in the lie that is promulgated in this physical universe—that things are what they seem. There is a certain fiction that passes for truth and usually it is perpetuated in an attempt to control or constrict by fear. It is prevalent in the human experience. Truth, however, is freedom from that outer oppression and hence, the inner oppression that we then create for ourselves. We must transcend the popular ideology of this human experience to see clearly, and we must do it trusting completely in the "I am" the teacher Jesus spoke of when he said, "I am the resurrection and the life." He was not referring to anything outside of himself. He was acknowledging the God within. "I of myself can do nothing. It is the Father within—the 'I am' that doeth the works."

It takes strength of character to transcend the popular notions and stand singularly (for ultimately our journey is a singular one) as a beacon of light in the midst of darkness. It is not a journey for the faint of heart. There is nothing equivocal about truth. It does not change day-to-day or moment-by-moment to suit a certain motive.

It is birthless, deathless, changeless, complete, perfect, whole and self-existent as Ernest Holmes tells us. Truth is the reason, cause and power in and through everything. Once we begin to see what is real, it becomes easy to see the illusion that is so much a part of everyday living. It becomes easy to see the way in which man has distracted himself from what is real and has bought into a false world in which everything is complicated. Truth is uncomplicated. It is simple. Life becomes simple for one who lives in truth. God simply is.

Affirmation:

I stand as a beacon of light undistracted by false reality! I emanate the "I am" presence within me! I say as the teacher Jesus said, "I am the resurrection and the life!"

Answering the Soul's Call

The Spirit within me is alive, awake and aware...I know that the all-wisdom guides me; the all-power protects me. The all-presence goes with me.

Ernest Holmes, *This Thing Called You*

The fear is fading into the background of my life. I am stepping out on faith and trust and walking the walk. I see that I've never been limited—only to the degree that I have chosen to limit myself. As I have answered my soul's call, my love for God and my awareness of God's love for me have deepened. What joy to walk in the depth of this love!

I now see so clearly the resistance and fear we humans live in every day, and how our culture feeds it. As we are able to transcend this human experience in consciousness, our physical bodies follow, and we are set free to live a whole new experience here in physical form. We begin to live as spiritual beings, not restricted by the mesmerism of the human condition.

We hold on so fiercely to our little lives as though it is all we have. In reality, the activity of our little lives is not even an appetizer to what God has in store for us. The great wealth that many of us pray for is not even the answer, for many with great wealth are locked in intense fear. It is rather an internal realization of the infinite supply of God as one's life—the realization of one's divine nature, one's holiness, and one's sacred identity that sets one free. It is not something attained on the outside. It is completely an inside job. With God, all things are possible; we live then in possibility consciousness.

God's love for you is so great; be willing to allow yourself to experience that! Step into the all-knowing consciousness of God. Be willing to let go, to slip into the swift current of God's love! Perfect joy and freedom await you there!

Affirmation:

I and my Father/Mother God are one! I am a divine expression of the Infinite! I am the resurrection and the life!

Enlarging Your Playing Field

Never hesitate to trust in that inner leading… We are all in the midst of Supreme Intelligence… We must be open to It at all times, ready to receive direction and to be guided into greater truths.

Ernest Holmes, *Creative Mind and Success*

Sometimes I can only tell who I am by looking back to see who I was. Who I am is constantly changing. I am emerging. We are all emerging from the smaller to the greater. I can look back and see the container of my life. Everything was done and all activity took place within the boundaries of the container. Right now in this present time and place, I see no boundaries, and my playing field has grown. I am comfortable in it. In fact, I would no longer be comfortable where I was. It would be like wearing a shoe that was one size too small.

This is the nature of spiritual evolution and our human experience of it. It is dynamic, and it is constantly moving. We step into the greater at the exact moment of readiness and not a moment sooner. I see all of the past as preparation for this present moment, which is the most glorious of all. Through it all, I grow closer to God and more aware of God's love for me. Through each step I take, I realize that the joy I feel is the joy of God realizing Itself within the flesh of my body.

I am in heaven on earth. I am expressing the fullness of God as my life. The love I feel is more intense; in fact, all of my experiences are richer and more fulfilling. The excitement of unlimited possibility courses through my veins. My faith and trust in God outweigh any fear, for I have set myself free. Do not be afraid. Let go and surrender now into your greatest yet to be. Sing your song as if your whole life depends upon it. It truly does!

Affirmation:

I step willingly onto my new playground! I fearlessly and joyously sing my song and dance my dance! God rejoices in Its beloved entertainer.

Soul Integrity

If we have to make a choice, we must be still in our own consciousness and know that the Spirit within knows... and will guide us.

Ernest Holmes, *The Science of Mind*

Integrity: The quality or state of being complete or undivided; completeness.

Webster's Seventh New Collegiate Dictionary

Integrity is not a fleeting thing; it is that by which our whole life is defined. Integrity is our bond of unification. The rules of conduct for our lives do not have to come from outside of us, though they often do because many of us are out of alignment with Source Energy which I call God. When we are in total alignment with Source Energy, we will automatically do what is for the highest and best for all living beings and ourselves.

Having your own personal integrity is what allows you to step into the great expansiveness of God's love. You must be willing to march to your own drumbeat. If you are caught up in pleasing the outside world and compromising your own inner knowing of what is right and true for you, you will never be able to get beyond your own individualized will into "Thy will be done." Ernest Holmes says, "Man does not exist for the purpose of making an impression upon his environment. He does exist to express himself in and through his environment. There is a great difference. It is not necessary that we leave any impression. It is not necessary, if we should pass on tonight, that anyone should remember that we have ever lived. All that means anything is that while we live, WE LIVE, and wherever we go from here, we shall keep on living. It is quite a burden lifted when we realize that we do not have to move the world—it is going to move anyway. This realization does not lessen our duty or our social obligation. It clarifies it. It enables us to do joyously, and free from morbidity, that which we should do in the social state."

Personal integrity is a day-by-day, moment-by-moment activity. You are the writer, director and the actor in your own play, but this play is not performed for the sake of the audience's pleasure. It is performed for your own joy!

Affirmation:

I surrender to the call of my Soul! I do not question my inner knowing for I recognize that I am one with God!

The Fire Within

Someday, after we have mastered the winds, the waves, the tides and gravity, we shall harness for God the energies of love. Then for the second time in the history of the world, man will have discovered fire.

Pierre Teilhard de Chardin

I have spent my life rushing around, constantly working, being busy, taking classes, and filling my life so full that I barely had time to breathe. The truth of the matter is I have been running away from myself. All that rushing around relieved me of the responsibility of being fully present and alive. It was a slow death and quite a socially accepted one to boot.

Now I sit in the midst of the fire. There is such passion burning within me. The passion is for life and living. The passion is for you to see who I truly am and for me to see who you truly are. The passion is for you to know how much I love you and for you to love me. The passion is for me to feel love beyond all fear and for me to somehow let you know how safe you are in the loving arms of God. This passion is consuming me now. It seems so self-absorbed that sometimes my human mind tries to judge it as not good—this absorption into self—but then I rest in the knowledge that my own unique path has brought me to this place. How could it not be the perfect place for me?

So I stop all the human activity and look within and what I see is unlimited possibility for me, for you, for all of us. This is truly living from the inside out, in perfect faith and trust in God. I let go now of the false belief that all that rushing around is going to make me safe in a complex world. I am safe in the midst of the silence of my own soul. I am safe in God. I am forever safe!

Affirmation:

The passion burns within me for love and for life! I open myself now to a brand new beginning! I am safe in the loving arms of God!

Beginning Again

Civilized people have lost the aptitude of stillness and must take lessons in silence from the wild before they are accepted by it.

Isak Dinesen, *Out of Africa*

On July 31, 2004, I started a walking safari in Africa. It turned out to be an initiation for me and the beginning of a spiritual journey that took me to various places around the world. I came home to myself in the motherland. My feet were on African soil and somehow I began again. I turned within to the stillness and became the perfect servant of my soul.

I set myself free. The love in me became greater than the fear. I let love lead the way instead of the fear I've known in the past. Love met love everywhere because that is the law of attraction. It is like being reborn with the innocence of a child but having the wisdom of the ages. The infinite of God is within each of us. We have access to all of it—the amazing wonder of it!

So much of the fear we live by is in the mind. Fear can paralyze us and make us do things we live forever to regret. Fear can cause us to hurt ourselves and others. Fear can keep us imprisoned in many ways; and we are run by that fear rather than being run by the love of God, which is our essential nature. There is no question that love is more powerful than fear. I have seen love in action. I have witnessed what love can do. Love is the answer to all the suffering and animosity in the world.

It is time to let go of the fear—to rise in God and in love and begin again. Once we do that, the doors to the kingdom of God open wide and abundant blessings fall upon us as though they were manna from heaven! We are set free!

Affirmation:

I am steeped in the love of God! My path is prepared before me! I meet love everywhere for I am love itself!

What Are You Willing?

In all spiritual disciplines, the opening wedge predicated for advancing one's awareness is described as willingness... A persistent willingness is the trigger that activates a new attractor field and allows one to begin to leave the old.

David R. Hawkins, M.D., Ph.D., *Power Vs Force*

In his book, David Hawkins postulates that there are levels of consciousness or energy fields and that each of us comes into the world at a certain energy level and rarely moves more than five points from that initial level of awareness during the course of his or her lifetime. He suggests that 85 percent of the world's population resides in the lower energy fields and only 4 percent of the population ever moves significantly from the lower levels of consciousness into the higher realms.

Will is a constantly repeated act of choice. One must make the constant choice for a greater level of awareness. The beauty of life is that we don't have to be stuck anywhere. We are supported and sustained by God as we move upward through the levels of awareness toward enlightenment. The only thing that stops us is our own lack of desire; the only thing that moves us forward is our intense willingness to experience more love, more joy, more peace and more freedom.

The desire to be one's true self is ever persistent. As we move into greater levels of awareness, our whole life experience changes. Where we once suffered pain, shame and guilt, we experience joy, peace and love. Where the world seemed to be against us, we now live in a world that supports us in every way. We attract more and more good into our lives because that's what love does. The great fear of everything slips away and what remains is infinite possibility. The joy is profound and the power of that kind of love significantly impacts the collective negativity in the world. One person who reaches the upper levels of enlightenment impacts the world significantly.

What are you willing? You are a creator, and you, individually, make a huge difference on the planet. God is love, and you are and always have been the great love of God. Be willing to see your true divinity!

Affirmation:

I am a place where the love of God is revealed on the planet!
I stand fearlessly in the power of the creator!

Living the Word

Wisdom is not assimilated with the eyes, but with the atoms.

Sri Yukteswar, quoted by Paramahansa Yogananda,

Autobiography of a Yogi

Finally I am living the words that I have spoken as a Science of Mind student these many years. The Word as Truth becomes the physical manifestation of the body and the body's affairs. Living the Word is absolute joy and absolute freedom. God as love awaits you everywhere. The Spirit of the Living God expresses in every moment of every day. I see that I have come to express peace, love and joy on the planet. We are not always even conscious of what we bring for it is our essential nature.

Two things begin to happen simultaneously. You attract at your level of consciousness and mainly good and positive things flow in your direction. Secondly, if challenges do arise (and they inevitably will in this human experience), you have the tools to use which will bring you back home to God and love. In your complete surrender to God in faith and trust, the Master Teacher lies within as the God Self. You become inner directed—not outer directed. Everything and nothing is familiar, for this is a transcended realm of existence. You are not caught up in race consciousness. You live the dream of infinite possibilities. This is living the Word—the authentic life. You walk in grace. Gratitude is your daily prayer. You seek nothing. There is no past and no future, only the present moment.

When the Word as Truth is our only reality, the ego must relinquish its playing field. There is no longer concern about how one shows up in the world for one is then listening and responding from the God within. There is nothing to prove to anyone. You are the proof.

So in this moment and every moment, I rest in the Word, knowing that I am forever safe. The love of God is my constant source and supply. It is my name and nature. I am filled with the spirit of joy and the expectancy of good things. My gratitude is overflowing.

Affirmation:

My life is the living embodiment of truth! I surrender all! I am the radiance, the purity and the perfection of the Omniscient One!

Holy Places; Holy Faces

Self-realization comes to us not by antagonizing or fighting other people's ways of believing, not by struggle or by strife, but by recognition—that is, by knowing the truth, by alignment with the nature of Reality which is wholeness and unity, goodness and beauty.

Ernest Holmes, *A Holmes Reader on Practical Wisdom*

My God is within me now. Love comes forth in a rich glow. It is as though I am the engineer on this train called life, and it is my job to stay on the tracks. Something or someone may come along which makes it difficult for me to stay present with love (I call it life), but I shall not be swayed from this heaven on earth. Everything and everyone is God, and we are all the same. Some of us are more awakened to our divinity; that is all. We are not meant to struggle in this existence but to live in the wholeness and purity of God's love. I do not choose disharmony when I can choose harmony. I welcome all my emotions as guideposts along the way to let me know where I'm presently standing. I do not live in a fairyland; I live on earth, but heaven can be found in the midst of anything. It is our job to recognize our own divinity and in that realization, to recognize the divinity in all others. Our clarity and conviction of truth then becomes a catalyst for others and for great transformation.

Self-realization is found in the silence of the soul. It is where I meet God, the eternal, immovable, transcendent One. As I slip into the silence, I meet the Eternal Lover, the One who does not judge me, the One who enables me to see beyond appearances, the One who quells any outward anxiety, the One who is my source and supply. How could I ever doubt what love has done for my life? How could I ever doubt God?

So I remain tuned in always to what is happening underneath the turbulence of life. It is from that place that all actions unfold. It is from that place that love recognizes itself everywhere and becomes defenseless. It is from that place that the answer to every question reveals itself. Holy places and holy faces are everywhere. Can you see them? They are awaiting your recognition.

Affirmation:

I rest in the inner tranquility of my soul! My God sustains me forever and always! I am what Thou art; Thou art what I am!

A Taste of Honey

*There is One Infinite Mind from which all things come...
Consequently, the Infinite is in and through man and is in and
through everything. Act as though I am and I will be.*

Ernest Holmes, *The Science of Mind*

So sweet and enduring is the love of God. If there is ever a slipping
backwards in my life into the forgetting, it is only momentary. That
is such good news, each day to be revealing more and more of my
true nature as Divine Spirit; but, of course, I see that I will never
get it done. I am better and better at loving myself and all others,
but there is no final destination in sight. How can there be? We are
talking about infinity.

I can see so clearly the fear and limitation and desire to control that
was my life and indeed the lives of many of us now. I can see all
the human contrivances we've developed out of nothing to keep us
safe—or so we thought. They are the very things now that we must
surrender in order to experience this heaven on earth—this supreme
taste of honey.

I have discovered that if you think you know, you know not.
Surrender is a willingness to live in the unknown. Letting go means
letting go of your need to be right or in control, even if that is the

only way you think you will be safe. It means letting go of your little ego. It means no longer focusing on what you call your "core issue" and focusing instead on how you can be more loving in your heart, desiring above all else to know your oneness with Divine Spirit. Is it worth it? Of course. Who does not want to live in paradise?

Sometimes I've wondered how I will ever be able to express in words what loving to this degree feels like, but then I know that I don't have to say a word. Each moment is a prayer, each day is a prayer, my life is a prayer. I can rest now. No more struggle; no more strife. Just grace and ease as I taste the sweet nectar of God's infinite love!

Affirmation:

Today and every day, I choose to express the love of God! Today and every day, I choose to experience heaven on earth! Today and every day, I taste the sweet nectar of joyous freedom!

My Soul Knoweth Right Well

The law is in the ground. You see that hill over there? Blackfellow Law like that hill. It never changes. Whitefellow Law goes this way, that way, all the time changing. Blackfellow Law different. It never changes. Blackfellow Law hard—like a stone, like that hill. The Law is in the ground.

Deborah Bird Rose, Aborigine, 1992

In the year 2005, I spent some time in Australia with the Aborigines. I celebrated my birthday while there and I called it my rebirthday. I wondered at the time what was so important to me about meeting the indigenous people everywhere I went in my travels—the Masai in Africa and the Aborigines in Australia. The Aborigines say that keeping alive the culture is not just for the old culture. "This for the goin' forward… It's not going back to the Stone Age; it's flowing our soul back to the beginning, the Dreaming, being one with the Presence of the Undying Spirit." And so I flow back to the Before, to the beginning, seeking only to know myself more fully, my oneness with God, my divinity. I willingly let go of the way things have been. In this life, I'm here to see it all differently. My Soul is my guide. It knows exactly what I need and how to deliver it to me. I do not question where I am to go or who I am to meet. I simply obey the call of my Soul, and I am delivered each day into more and more light. As I behold the face of God everywhere, the face of God shows up. As I let go of judgment, there is more to love in everyone. People miraculously transform before my eyes. Is it them or me who has changed? It doesn't matter.

It is clear that my interior life has activated what is happening in my outer experience. The real me is emerging—the me that only wants to love and be loved. This is what happens when one surrenders completely to God, wanting only to know oneness and unity with all of life. What used to be important is just not important anymore. I am being birthed into my True Identity. That reality is showing itself in every aspect of my life. It is a life of grace and ease and everyday miracles. I am set free to live life more fully, more joyfully, and more abundantly!

Affirmation:

My life is the life of God! Joyously, I see as God sees! I am free to be my authentic Self!

Thanks Giving

Every good gift and every perfect gift is from above…

Holy Bible, James 1:17

I thank you, Dear Spirit, for loving me even when I cannot love myself. I thank you for guiding me when I've lost my way. I thank you for all the miracles, seen and unseen, that have brought me back into alignment with my true nature. I thank you for placing before me so many opportunities to learn love for myself so that I could learn to love others.

I thank you, Dear Creator, for the outstanding beauty of nature that makes me so appreciate life. I thank you for the wisdom to make the right choices for my good. I thank you, Dear God, for the vigor and health of my body that allows me to experience such a joyful, active life. I thank you for the sunrises and sunsets, for the vastness of the ocean and the beauty of its many moods and colors. I thank you for the roof over my head and the delicious food I get to eat. I thank you for all the loving beings that surround me.

I thank you for the quiet moments of self reflection, for the peace in my heart when I realize how much I am loved. Thank you for the clothes on my back and my faithful car that takes me wherever I want to go. Thank you for the people and books that inspire me, for roses that smell heavenly, for kindred spirits that understand me and support me in my life's journey.

Thank you for the way my vibration is lifted when I speak of my blessings. Thank you for the fact that more blessings come to me when I appreciate the ones I have. Thank you for this benevolent universe. Thank you for my life!

Affirmation:
I shall make every day a day to give thanks!

Katrina (The God View)

The hope of glory is your awareness of the ability to rise perpetually to higher levels.

Neville, *The Power of Awareness*

I have a picture in my mind of the man who was interviewed on TV while hooking up his small boat to the back of his truck. He was about to head for Louisiana. He said, "Well, all I know is that if my wife and child were there, I would want someone like me to show up." He was not asking for permission; he was listening and following his heart. He said he was no hero, just a red-necked etc. etc. (his words, not mine). The cameras went on to show his efforts later, pulling people to safety in his small boat. Though on the macrocosmic level, nothing was happening; on the microcosmic level, a lot was happening. This man and so many others during this crisis were feeling something on a personal level. They knew the right thing to do and did it.

This is what we mean when we say if you want peace and love on earth, then become the peace and love you wish to see. Something shifted when people realized that they would have to do it themselves. They listened to their inner urgings and followed their hearts. They did not ask permission. They did what was right. The transformation on the planet will and is taking place in just that way—it is happening on the microcosmic level and cannot help but create a new tomorrow on the macrocosmic level. It is the power of love, the power of the open heart—the most powerful force on earth.

Behold, I make all things new. A spotlight is shown upon the areas needing great healing. No matter the spin put upon the story, it is clear for all to see—the body floating face down in the water for days—an image that will remain with me for a long time. Behold, I make all things new. Sometimes it is only through pain and devastation that the message gets through. It is a powerful message supported by a powerful force. Behold, I make all things new.

Affirmation:

I am a place of transformation on the planet! I am a powerful force for good! I open my heart to everyone and everything!

The Power of Prayer

...whereas I was blind, now I see.

Holy Bible, John 9:25

Do know this. As we are listening, our Beloved God is listening and responding immediately if we can but remove all resistance. We are living in a universe that answers all our needs if we are willing to allow. I pray every day to remind myself of who I am and the Power that indwells me. Though I am in this physical body, I desire to live each and every moment seeing as God sees. Sometimes (or even often) I need a reminder to get me back on track. How blessed and grateful I am for my prayer partners who always see me as God sees me. I've discovered their preciousness in my life. The power of our prayers as we unite together has been proven to me over and over again.

All of us have chosen to live in a physical universe filled with challenges, distractions and constant change. To walk through this world, living in harmony, peace, joy and love requires constant awareness and a willingness to continue asking, "Who do I need to become in this situation to stay in my loving?" My prayers and their prayers keep bringing me back to myself, back to the truth that sets me free, back to remembering who I am as a divine being. With the constancy of our prayers together, I am daily lifted out of the mesmerism of this human experience. I can see beyond appearance and release all resistance. Gradually and gratefully, it is becoming a way of life for me—to be more concerned with being loving than with being right or even heard, for sometimes the physical friends I meet along the path just need to be listened to; and it is really so little to ask of me.

God is so good, I tell you. I am constantly restored by prayer, and my prayers are always answered. Love reigns supreme in my life; the desire in my heart is so strong. Have you prayed today? God is always responding, always loving you. It is the blessed gift of life.

Affirmation:

Thank you, God, for I know my prayers are always answered! I am tuned in, and tapped into the Divine! I radiate loving acceptance everywhere I am!

Now—the Creative Field

When you make friends with the present moment, you feel at home no matter where you are. When you don't feel at home in the Now, no matter where you go, you will carry unease with you.

Eckhart Tolle, *Stillness Speaks*

My life is so joy-filled and rich now in each and every moment as I travel all over the world, being in new places and meeting new people. I have no plans for the future and I'm not very interested in my past, so I find myself constantly living in the precise moment of Now.

Eckhart Tolle says the division of life into past, present and future is mind-made and ultimately illusory. Past and future are thought forms, mental abstractions. So what are we then left with that is real—only this precise, precious moment that you are in right now as you read this. This is the moment, the Now, of your real living, the only place where life exists! It is in the Now moment that your thoughts slow down and you begin to truly see and experience the oneness of all life, to appreciate God's creation in its fullness and radiance. What you do in the present moment is the creative seed for your future! I've wasted most of my life living in the past or anticipating the future. That is not where the joy is. The joy is right now in the amazing intensity of each and every moment.

When I am present in the Now, I am completely with you. I am not a million miles away. I'm seeing you. I'm joining with you. I'm hearing you. I have nothing else on my mind but what you are saying to me. I am firmly rooted in my Being. I am aware of who I am and who you are as a divine being, and I respond from a place of infinite awareness.

Gratefully and thankfully, I am being born again into a fresh, new way of fearless living and loving. I do not dwell in the past or worry about the future. I am creating it right now in this precious moment, and each and every experience with another is a holy encounter!

Affirmation:

I am not my thoughts. I am life itself! I am the space in which all things happen. I am consciousness. I am the Now. I am!

Who Chooses?

Choice implies consciousness–a high degree of consciousness. Without it, you have no choice. Choice begins the moment you disidentify from the mind and its conditioned patterns, the moment you become present.

Eckhart Tolle, *The Power of Now*

Jesus said, "Forgive them for they know not what they do." Until we wake up, we are being run by our unconscious minds. We are not making choices based on our awareness of who we are as spiritual beings. Given that, can't we then more easily forgive our mother, father, sister, brother or others who have harmed us when we realize that their decisions were made from the darkness, not the light? Can't we more easily forgive them when we realize that, for all intents and purposes, they really did not have a choice? They were responding from a mind-based identity that was already conditioned from the past. No one would willingly choose such pain, suffering and dysfunction.

The one who is truly choosing is the one who has awakened to his or her true identity as Divine Being. It is from this place that we can then choose to forgive all those who are yet in darkness, all those who have not yet realized who they are. It is from this place that judgment is released and true compassion is born. Eckhart Tolle says to relinquish judgment does not mean that you do not recognize dysfunction and unconsciousness when you see it. It means being the knowing rather than being the reaction and the judge.

So who is choosing? Are you choosing or are you caught up in your egoic mind-identity? Living from the awakened life is not easy. There will always be someone or something to judge. There will always be someone or something to criticize and condemn. As for myself, there but for the grace of God go I. I was once in darkness. Would you be able to forgive me? Would you be able to see me as God sees me now and has always seen me? That, my Beloveds, is the challenge. That is what we have come here to do—simply, to love and be loved, to forgive and forget!

Affirmation:

I am present moment awareness! I forgive and forget, knowing that it is the way to love! Compassion is born in me, and I am set free!

The Changeless

If you can see God in everything, then God will look back at you through everything. When the time comes that nothing goes forth from you other than that which you would be glad to have return, then you will have reached your heaven.

Ernest Holmes, *This Thing Called You*

It is fruitless to try to change the people or situations around us. All we can change is our own thinking and behavior about them. I sit in the midst of a situation that seems to need change and concentrate on me, on how I can stay centered in my oneness and be a place where love reveals itself. Then things change, but have they changed or have I changed? Something definitely is different. Who has changed?

The more I try to change things or resist them or argue against them, the more separation I feel. In my separation, I cannot possibly be a force for good. I only create more separation. It is not my job to fix anything. There is nothing that needs fixing. We cannot know another's path or destiny. It is my job to stay in my own business, to stay connected to God, the source of all supply, to stay in my oneness with all of life. From there, I can be a beneficial presence on this planet.

There will always be some issue or someone to fight against or be in resistance to, and right there we must begin our work—the work of right thinking and right seeing—God's work. Science of Mind has given us wonderful tools to use and principles to practice, and we must practice them every day to stay at peace in a chaotic world. Our spiritual work is our salvation. The mystery of life unfolds before us. Why them? Why now? Why that? And we rest in the deep assurance that God is with us constantly, keeping us safe, guiding and directing us every step of the way. With God as my guiding light, anything is possible! I look forward to the miracles!

Affirmation:

I am a place of peace on the planet! I accept and allow the grace of God to carry me! I am a beneficial presence for good!

Resurrection

It is the intellect and the subconscious self which needs renewing. The Spirit neither sleeps nor slumbers. The Spirit is God.

Ernest Holmes, *This Thing Called You*

Rise up, my Beloveds, rise up! The time has come to rise up. Heaven on earth awaits you. You can choose differently. Freedom is just a thought away.

Choose to let acceptance and peace run your life instead of pain and suffering. Choose to love and to be connected with all of life instead of constantly being in judgment of people and situations, which only takes you into separation. Choose joy and optimism instead of unhappiness and negativity. Choose freedom and expansion instead of bondage to your limited ideas! All of this is just a difference in thinking. No matter what your situation, you can choose thoughts that will transform your circumstance. In fact, that is how miracles are manifested—by a daring, new thought!

During this month, take charge of your life in a new way. Give up your pity party. Decide today that you are going to live from the precious life of God that indwells you. Decide today that you are the master of your fate and no one else has control over you. You are a co-creator with God. The more you wake up and become aware of that truth, the more heaven on earth you will experience and the more miracles you will witness in your everyday life.

I know this is true because I am living it. Every day I have the opportunity to make a million choices. Through experience, I've learned to make conscious choices that enhance my sense of well being, that enhance my peace and joy, and that move me into greater love and acceptance. I do not choose to feel bad; and when that does arise, I choose a new thought or a new way of being that will return me to my peace, joy, love, forgiveness and compassion. I choose beauty, grace and wholeness! I choose God!

Affirmation:

Every day in every way, I consciously choose my good! I expand my consciousness into the realm of infinite possibility! I choose life! I choose love! I choose God!

The Sacred Word

The great word is not a word, as many suppose, nor a definite statement of truth. The great word is the soul of every word, the spirit of every thought and the inner power of every expressed statement.

Christian D. Larson, *The Pathway of Roses*

I've been thinking about the word and what makes the spoken word powerful. We, as practitioners of truth, speak our word in the form of prayer treatments for our clients. My prayers have changed over the years but not necessarily the words I speak. What has changed is what I now know, compared to what I used to hope was true. Now I know the truth about you and all of us as spiritual beings; and whether I speak a word about it or not, the energetic of what I know is the vibration that carries us all higher into the realm of infinite possibility. I cannot be fooled or deceived by even your own idea of a lesser being living its life as you. I see the miracle of you. I see the transcendent reality of your life and the perfection that is within you. When I speak about you, the reality I see and know without a doubt is what is transmitted to you by the very vibration of my being. It is the message of God being transmitted to you, about you, through me. What a blessing it is to sit before my own practitioner and feel the presence of God and the love of God washing over me. No words even need to be spoken.

As my belief, faith and trust have grown and deepened, my word has become more sacred and more powerful—not because in my early days as a practitioner, my words were not always true—but because now I know, beyond a shadow of a doubt, that they are true. What a blessing to know the truth and be resolute on where I stand in the midst of it.

No, you cannot sway me. I cannot be deceived even by the ways in which you have deceived yourself. The illumined life is your life! It is the life God has ordained for you as its creation. It is a magnificent life, filled with promise, freedom, joy, abundance, love, compassion, beauty, perfection and wholeness. Step into it now. Live and love fearlessly!

Affirmation:

I step eagerly into this new day! I embrace myself as a Divine Being!

Timeless Awareness

Thrust in thy sickle and reap; for the time is come for thee to reap; for the harvest of the earth is ripe.

Holy Bible, Rev. 4:15

Ah, paradise is here—even in the mundane. Paradise is here in the freedom. Paradise is here in the love. Paradise is truly here, and I am no longer run by fear.

Oh, how much I needed to be in control of my life. Nothing was left to guesswork. I had a plan, and I always followed through. I must say I was successful, but not in the way I am today. Today is different. I don't have a plan—at least not a long-range one.

Now I am open to infinite possibility. I'm not running my life any more. God has taken over, and it is so much easier. My energy is not the mind energy that has created our current world, but instead spiritual energy, which vibrates at a higher level. My doing is now infused with Being, and it is a joyful celebration. There is a divine plan for my life. I follow the inner urgings, not my mind's urging but my heart's urging; and there I find freedom such as I've never known—love, compassion, non-judgment and peace.

To the outside world, it looks as though I've lost my mind. In a manner of speaking, I have, but I give little thought to my self-image. I see the illusion we live in that we call reality—all man-made contrivances to keep us distracted and anti-bored. Underneath all that subterfuge, life is so simple.

My life has greater meaning than ever before now that my ego, which consists largely of resistance, is no longer in charge. I am Being, and Being is a gift to the planet. It is a wake-up call. My love has surpassed my fear, and the fearful ones are attracted to the fearless. God is my source and supply. I am in paradise. My only wish is to be joined by my brothers and sisters. They are coming, I know; and I await them with a joyful heart.

Affirmation:

I surrender all to Thee! Lead me, Divine One, into righteousness! I abide under the shadow of the Almighty! My cup runneth over!

Inspired Living

Whatever you may think of the question of free will, the truth is your experiences throughout your life are determined by your assumptions—whether conscious or unconscious.

Neville, *The Power of Awareness*

"That where you have been in imagination, there you will be in the flesh also." (Neville) You can lay all the groundwork you want in the physical, but if you do not believe in the outcome or if you cannot imagine yourself in that outcome, it will not come to pass. How could I have failed, you say. I have done everything necessary to succeed, but the truth is you could not see yourself there in the vision. The most powerful moment of creation is in consciousness, often well before anything is ever seen in the physical realm. This is valuable information for it teaches us the importance of the work done in the stillness of our own soul. The closer your vision is to the deep desires of your heart, the easier it will be to see yourself in it and to believe in what you see in mind. What is it you deeply desire to express and share as your life's work? In what way have you shown up in the flesh to serve? What is it your heart is pulling you to do, and can you see yourself doing it? Can you feel the joy in you as you do it? We came here to live inspired, passionate, purposeful lives—not to just drag ourselves through each day, only to wake up to another unfulfilling, uninspired one tomorrow.

These are powerful times. Change is going on all around us. We are living in a constantly evolving universe. We are an important part of God's plan. We came not to waste our lives. We came to be joyous, to be loving, to give our gifts. God supports us 100% when we step out to give the gift we came to give. We have all that we need in time and on time. See yourself living an inspired life, filled with passion and purpose! Feel it, sense it, and know it for yourself. Then watch it manifest in physical form. It is your divine destiny!

Affirmation:

I see myself living my dream! I am inspired and passionate! My divine purpose for being is fulfilled!

Courageous Living

This body is not me. I am not limited by this body. I am life without boundaries.

Thich Nhat Hanh

Courage is fear confronted. It is stepping through rather than fleeing from. It is facing the darkness until you see the light. Courage is dissolving everything you've ever known into one irreconcilable truth: You can surmount any obstacle placed before you, no matter the seeming difficulty. Courage is not for the faint of heart; it is for the brave and bold heart, and every heart has the capacity for bravery and boldness. Courage takes accessing our personal power—that which is limitless because its source is divine. Courage takes letting go of limited thinking. It takes letting go of the perceived failures and mistakes of the past, as you defined them.

I behold in you great things, saith the Lord. I behold in you great power and great strength. I behold in you great wisdom and great courage. Take heart, my Beloveds, for you are in my care. I shall never desert you. You are my Beloved. I have created you out of myself. Your strength is my strength. Your power is my power. Your love is my love. Your joy is my joy. I am witness to the greatness in you. I am witness to the beauty in you. I am witness to the light in you. I have created you out of myself. Be courageous in the sight of whatever faces you. I shall not desert you. You are with and of me forever and ever. These are my words to you. This is my love for you. Your greatness is in my eyes. You are my light and my love. I am with you always.

Affirmation:

The courage of God is my courage! The strength of God is my strength! I behold the greatness in myself for I am what Thou art; Thou art what I am!

The Triumphant Life

Where love is, there will the light be also; and neither darkness, sickness nor sin can exist in the light.

Christian D. Larson, *The Pathway of Roses*

Recently I experienced a dark night of the soul. Even in the midst of it, I knew on some level that it would ultimately take me deeper into the realization of the Divine Self that is the center of my being. It required me to stay in the loving no matter what was coming at me. I began to see so clearly the power of love. I realize now that nothing is more powerful than the love inside of me. Everything unlike God dissolves in the face of it. Attack, anger and fear dissolve in the face of it. The challenge is to stay in the loving, no matter what is coming your way. If you can do that, everything in the outer world shifts. All that remains is oneness and peace.

I choose love, and in that is my freedom. I am no longer willing to dwell in unpleasant feelings of any kind. I want to feel good—to feel joyous, so that is what I am choosing. It is not complicated. In fact, it is quite simple. It is taking charge of your life and your experience in a way you perhaps have never done before. I am testimony to the fact that love is the most powerful force on the planet. I see it every day in every way. As you choose greater and greater love as your dominant vibration, what a healing force you become on the planet.

Everyone is affected by the energetic of love. It is captivating. More and more love comes to you as one who chooses love as the primary expression.

It is time to choose love, peace and harmony instead of anger, resentment and hostility. Embrace forgiveness, forgiving yourself and all others. Each moment is precious. Don't waste it. Let love be the dominant force in your life and watch your life change into one of blessing, prosperity, peace and harmony. You deserve it, and the time is now!

Affirmation:

I open my heart and express all the love I am! I forgive myself and all others, knowing it will set me free! I live the triumphant life of God!

From Within

To be perfectly satisfied to let your light shine wherever you may go without ever looking back to see if there were results or no, is the mark of a great soul.

Christian D. Larson, *The Pathway of Roses*

You cannot count on someone else's opinion of you to give you a sense of your own worth. I used to be so concerned about other peoples' opinions of me. I used to wait for, and then hang on to, a good word spoken about me for then, and only then, did I know my value in the world. Something has changed.

Now I have called myself to such a high standard of livingness and lovingness, that there is no one in the world whose opinion of me is more important than my own. As we become more loving in our hearts, it is that love that is the guiding force in all we do. It is that love that asks whether what I've done is the loving thing to do and works daily toward nonjudgment of self and others. It is that love that assures me of my own worthiness and value in a world of conflicting and ever-changing values.

Where did I meet that love? How did I find it? I found it in prayer and meditation in the silence of my own soul. There is where I meet God. There is where the Holy Communion began and where

I first realized how much God loves me, and indeed loves all of its creation. It is there where I began to understand that God is always ultimately my source and supply, no matter the appearance of it in the human realm. It is there that I came to really love myself as God loves me and to daily work to love others as myself as Jesus admonished us to do.

It is so freeing to march to the beat of one's own drum and yet to know that my drumbeat is the heartbeat of the universe and the eternal life of God. I cannot go wrong as I turn within and listen to the messages and guidance of my Beloved God. I have been set free!

Affirmation:

I let go of all limited thinking! I dive deep into the silence of my own soul! I let go and allow myself to love and be loved!

Sacred Sight

It is written that God is Love, and that we are His expressed likeness, the image of the Eternal Being. Love is self-givingness through creation, the impartation of the Divine through the human.

Ernest Holmes

The Science of Mind, From the Teachings of Jesus

Throughout my travels over the past years, I have been visiting indigenous peoples and sacred sites all over the world, and I have discovered that the sacred is always within my sight. I don't have to travel far to see it. I open my eyes. The sacred is everywhere. It's about choosing to see differently.

I was in a car accident a few years back; it was my fault. Today I think of that event as a wonderful sacred day in my life. To some it would only be remembered as a catastrophe. I was so concerned and expressed so much love to the person I hit (fortunately no one was injured), that love came back to me over and over again during the day as my brand new car was taken in for repairs. I was supplied so beautifully by everyone in such a loving way all throughout the day. I remember thinking at the end of that day, as I lay down to sleep, what a blessed day I had just experienced and how much love I had received. It was a car accident, but I yielded to love and grace

Barbara

experience of everyone involved with

when you can yield to love? Why choose

choose surrender to a greater idea and way

most powerful force on the planet? It is

control and to be right that causes us to

es of love, allowing peace to prevail

is transcended Being. Sacred sight is

to a greater idea than what appears on

the surface. So as we go forward into each new day, let us open our eyes to the sacred that is everywhere before us. We choose to see God and the activity of God everywhere, no matter the seeming appearance of separation, and we are overcome by God's grace. We behold God's sacred sites everywhere with our sacred sight.

Affirmation:

I open my eyes to see that love is everywhere. I turn away from thoughts and actions of separation. I enter the domain of the kingdom of God and therein I dwell.

Let Freedom Ring!

If a man takes his images of thought only from his previous experiences, then he continues in the bondage which those previous experiences create.

Ernest Holmes, *The Science of Mind*

Let's spend this beautiful month freeing ourselves from the bondage of our own limited thinking! We were not born for struggle and strife. We were born into this physical expression to have life and have it abundantly, so break loose the shackles that are holding you captive to your own faulty thinking. The riches and blessings of the kingdom are awaiting you when you finally let go of all resistance to receiving them.

Some of us, underneath it all, do not feel deserving enough to be so blessed. How can that possibly be so? You are an amazing creation of God. That alone makes you worthy. Some of us don't want to let go of control. We are just sure that we are right, and they are wrong. The truth is that it is all a judgment, and who is judging. So you get to stand in your judgment, totally separated from the love you seek!

We are creating all the time, consciously or unconsciously. The question is, what are we creating? As we become more and more conscious, we can create what we want, rather than what we don't want. No one said creating consciously would be easy. So many negative fear-based thoughts can creep in when we are not vigilant, but fortunately we have a guidance system that lets us know, through what we are feeling, that we are off track. If we want to live a joy-filled life, it is then our opportunity to bring our thoughts back into alignment with our desires.

I love this process of conscious creation. It is exciting to see what shows up when our thoughts move into alignment with our desires. The universe is just waiting to deliver the goods. All that is ever in the way is our own resistance. So today and every day, we open our minds and hearts and let ourselves fly free in Spirit! We were born to fly free!

Affirmation:

I willingly release all resistance, doubt and confusion! I embrace all that I am as a conscious co-creator with God! I live and love fearlessly!

Unleashing Your Magnificent Self

Safety is the most unsafe spiritual path you can take. Safety keeps you numb and dead. People are caught by surprise when it is time to die. They have allowed themselves to live so little.

Stephen Levine, *The Mindful Soul*

Living largely is an adventure in courage, faith and trust! One is no longer controlled by the little egoic mind that seeks security and sameness. When I talk about living largely, I'm not even talking about a huge life change. I'm talking about a shift in consciousness, but be aware that a shift in consciousness often will bring about a huge life change!

What is the shift in consciousness to which I'm referring? It is a willingness to come out from among them, to become your own person, to live from the inside out with a willingness to follow your own inner guidance, to not fall prey to the palpable and numerous fear messages that are in the ethers all around us. It is a new way of being in the world, but not of it. You are your own person, uniquely you, like no other on the face of the earth, having come here to express your unique God-given gifts fearlessly and boldly. It is a shift in consciousness that says you are not alone, that you live in a benevolent universe and are connected to everything. What you do and what you say matters. It is a shift in consciousness that enables you to recognize that you are the love you've been seeking, and your primary purpose for being is to express that love.

It appears sometimes as though you are going in the opposite direction of everyone else, but there is something within you that knows your direction is the perfect one for you. You have witnessed the miracles already and the payoff of complete surrender. It seems like you have no choice any more but to follow; the joy is so profound. Now this is really living; and I, for one, will know it before I die.

God's love is upon us so profoundly. How could we have ever doubted it? I witness the beauty all around me and my heart sings with joy. I am truly free!

Affirmation:

Profound joy lights up my life! I radiate peace and love everywhere! I am what I've been seeking! I am! I am!

The Bird is the Word!

When the book about the bird and the bird disagree, listen to the bird.

Rev. David Leonard

RSI Ministerial Intensive, Asilomar, July 2006

This adventure in faith or God is a heart experience, so much more than merely a head experience. Rev. Leonard's statement has been a theme in my life. It is about listening preferentially to the still small voice within rather than the messages of the outer world. It is about self mastery. It is about truly believing that I and my Father are one; and because of that, I have access to divine truth and wisdom. Though we speak those words, it is quite another matter to embody them to the degree that we are willing to stand out from the crowd and march to our own drumbeat.

As Ernest Holmes tells us "No man need go unguided through life, for all are divine at the center and all are Images of the Most High!" Jesus, the great mystic, is a perfect example of one who listened within. He communed with his own soul to the extent that he realized his connection to God. He realized his own divinity and I-AM-NESS; and through his own willingness, became a place where God could express in human form. He believed in God in himself, and he knew the same truth for each of us.

There comes a time in the course of our spiritual evolution when the only voice we can trust is the one that is within each of us. It is because our path is so unique. No one else can possibly know what is for our highest good. No one else can possibly know what course we need to take in order to receive the greatest blessing.

Only by penetrating deeper and deeper into our own soul can we know the reality of our own I-AM-NESS. Only by listening in the stillness can we meet God, the Beloved Creator. Everything is within us—the ability to know, the ability to heal, the ability to love unconditionally. Heaven is within each of us!

Affirmation:

I surrender now into the stillness of my own soul! I know that I and my Father are one! I trust completely in my own divine nature for I am made in the image and likeness of God!

Abundance Consciousness

Life is ever giving of Itself. We must receive, utilize and extend the gift. Success and prosperity are spiritual attributes belonging to all people, but not necessarily used by all people.

Ernest Holmes, *The Science of Mind*

The boundaries about what is mine and what is yours are less rigid than they used to be. In the big scheme of things, the resources of this planet belong to everyone. I want to say then that no one should die of hunger, but they do. I find that the looser I am with my own resources, the more blessings come my way. The tighter my grip on what I perceive to be mine, the more constricted I feel and the more the wellspring of divine flow dries up.

Giving comes in many forms such as being a good listener to someone who needs to be heard, showing up for someone in pain, sending a card to express your gratitude, and saying "I love you" whenever you know it is true. There are innumerable ways of giving your resources. The greatest way to move beyond the feelings and expectations of lack is to become a giver, being dedicated to expressing that givingness from the heart (without thought of reward) every day and as many times during each day as possible. It is a life-changing activity of selfless service. This is what we do when we show up as the vessel through which God's love can be known and felt. I believe it is our true purpose for being.

If we continue to hold on so tightly and desperately, whether in physical form or in mind, to what we think is ours, it restricts the divine flow of resources which are ever and ever circulating in the universe. What I know is that the gifts of the kingdom are constantly pouring forth; and if we do not restrict or resist them, those gifts will easily and effortlessly be ours. So we open ourselves to our ever-expanding good and give of ourselves and our gifts as though our divine life depended upon it. It does!

Affirmation:

I give from the wellspring of my good! I give generously and gratefully! I am an instrument through which God's love is known and felt!

Tending the Garden of Gratitude

When our consciousness is lifted to that sense of "Thank you, Father; thank you, everyone," then comes the fullness and completeness of communion with God, and in that there is a resting in the Soul.

Joel S. Goldsmith, *The Art of Spiritual Healing*

How could I have known that there was so much to be grateful for? It didn't seem like it even twenty years ago. It's certainly not about material things. I appear to have less of that than ever. It's something else that permeates my whole body—sort of a joyful sense of awareness about who I am and the beauty and perfection all around me. Sometimes the beauty is covered up a little, like the plants in the garden I'm working in. They looked all sad and hopeless, having been little tended, but as I trim and touch them and give them my love and attention, their beauty is revealed so amazingly—like we humans who just need to be seen in our perfection. It's not a complicated idea. It's really very simple.

The more I behold the perfection, the more it shows up and the more grateful I am. I've discovered that in those areas where I feel separation (yes, it happens; I'm human), if I cultivate that area with a little love and attention, just like in the garden, I don't feel separate any more. I feel connected to that person, place or thing. The tension eases, my being feels at peace and more gratitude surfaces. I'm tending my own inner garden. I'm not waiting around for someone else to do it. I want to feel the joy that comes from doing it myself and right now, not later.

It's another way in which we take responsibility for our lives and how we feel and how our lives are working for us. There is always an opportunity to cultivate and sew new seeds of love and appreciation. There is always an opportunity to shine the light of truth.

I look forward to working in my garden for I see that I do reap what I sew. I am grateful to be an instrument on the planet whereby more beauty and truth get revealed!

Affirmation:

My heart is filled with joy as I cultivate my inner garden! Gratitude washes over me for I see the Beloved everywhere!

Jesus, the Man, the Mystic

Again Jesus spoke to them, saying, I am the light of the world;
he who follows me shall not walk in darkness, but he shall find
for himself the light of life.

Holy Bible, Lamsa Translation, St. John 8:12

There was a simple man who lived some 2000 years ago. He was
not a Messiah in his time, but rather a maker of spoons and bowls.
He traveled in a radius of about 100 miles with a group of followers
of scarce means. There was something so extraordinary about him,
however, that to this day, we are still learning from his teachings.
For me, his life is a great inspiration primarily because he was a
simple man of flesh and bone, and yet there was something he knew
about himself that gave him great power as a way-shower and truth
teller.

What did he know about himself that we can know about ourselves?
He knew that he was a creation of God. He knew that he had direct
access to the Divine. He talked to God and was answered. He did
not ever doubt his worthiness, nor did he doubt his role to speak
the truth. We are all the Beloved of God. We are inspired by the
great ones who have gone before us and the great ones that are on
the planet now, but we are never less than they. There is the same
capacity for greatness in each of us. There is the same capacity to

leave a great legacy, but leaving a great legacy should never be our focus. Jesus did not even know the impact he would have on the world during his lifetime. He just followed his inner urgings, mostly inspired by God.

Let us celebrate our own birth into a greater awareness of our Divine identity as a beloved creation of God. Let us be givers, not just of material goods, but of the love within us. Let us celebrate by revealing and expressing the love we seek.

Affirmation:

I reveal and express all the love I am! I allow the light of God to illuminate my Being! I radiate the joy of God everywhere I am!

A New Year, A New You

Happy is the man that findeth wisdom and the man that getteth understanding.

Holy Bible, Prov. 3:13

The all-consuming love of God is at hand. It can fuel your life. I thought I knew everything; but once again, I'm a student, learning how to live in this world but not of it. It is a constant daily practice, and I thank God that I am not alone.

Every day, I practice staying centered in my own truth when the world around me and the people in it seem to be living on another page of the book of life. The challenge is to continue to express my love and realize my connection even when sometimes I feel so far apart from the other one before me. I know that I would not be able to do it without a daily spiritual practice—meditation, reading and prayer. This kind of open-hearted, moment-by-moment living does not just come from attending church on Sunday; it comes from a dedicated desire and intention to be more loving in my heart.

Living this way has become easier and easier because I've retrained my mind to think different thoughts—most of the time, they are thoughts that produce a good feeling of joy and peace within me. The payoff is enormous. I get to be happy and feel good most of the time, and people like to be around a happy person. I think sometimes that we humans are searching in the wrong direction for our happiness, and then it is so disappointing when it doesn't come.

The simpler my life, the happier I've become. The great ones whom we've admired the most lead pretty simple lives! Maybe there is a lesson in that.

Affirmation:

I realize everyday joy in everyday things! I promote peace and happiness everywhere I go! In the name of love, I willingly let go of my need to be right!

Miracle Consciousness

There is a point in the supreme moment of realization where the individual merges with the universe... It is here that the mentality performs seeming miracles, because there is nothing to hinder the whole from coming through.

Ernest Holmes, *The Science of Mind*

A few years ago, I was in Denver, Colorado, in the midst of a major snow storm. I was to fly back to Los Angeles the following day. It didn't look like any planes would fly the next day and maybe not for several days. Another storm was on its way. At first my reaction was the typical human reaction—that the situation was a small disaster. Where would I stay? How and when would I ever get a plane out, etc., but then as I entered meditation and prayer the following morning, I had a powerful realization. We are always, and I mean always with no exception, exactly where we are supposed to be. The minute I came to that realization, I began to see the situation in a totally different light. The scene outside became a winter wonderland. A peace came over me. If I'm in Denver instead of where I had planned to be in Los Angeles, what awaits me then in Denver? Who will I meet? What will transpire in the next few days? In my acceptance, all was well. I could now show up as love in Denver, Colorado, and behold the miracle of God's love! I was free of all encumbrances and of all resistance—a perfect place for God to express as me!

As I moved into this consciousness of complete acceptance of what is, I realized that I had now also created the perfect atmosphere for my plane to fly out of Denver to Los Angeles. I had removed all resistance to what is. I had created the opportunity for a miracle. The next day, though flights were cancelled all morning, planes due to fly out after 12:00 p.m. were on schedule. My plane flew out at 1:43 p.m.

We are always exactly in the right place at the right time! We are emissaries of the Divine—never less than that. It serves us not to be in resistance to anything for God is everywhere!

Affirmation:

I willingly and freely let go of all resistance to anything! I allow myself to show up as infinite love! I am surrounded by the beauty of God's creation!

Emergence

Spiritual experience… cannot—and does not—borrow its light from another, no matter how great or noble that other may be. It springs from within, coming from that never-failing fountain of life, which quenches every thirst, whose Source is in eternity; the well-spring of self-existence.

Ernest Holmes, *The Science of Mind*

A new, magnificent you is emerging now. It is unstoppable. You have willed it so by all you've done up to this present moment.

This new you is willing to live and love fearlessly and to be bold in stating and living its truth. It is not fueled by the same desires of earlier days, but rather by the deeper, purer desires of the heart. It is fueled by the desire to love and be loved, to serve and be served, and the desire to be beauty and see beauty everywhere. It has transcended all the false beliefs about the way to happiness or peace. It lives in utter and complete prosperity and abundance, knowing its source and supply is unlimited. It is not afraid to be seen and heard, and it listens so much more intensely. It hears everything spoken and unspoken. It hears beyond the words being said.

This new you is filled with joy. Joy bubbles up over the simplest of things. It wants to share and give and be in surroundings that nurture its soul. It is humble in its greatness, realizing that something else has arisen within which is not ego-driven. It is driven by the pure desire of perfect love and service!

The new you has the energy and vitality to do whatever is at hand. It answers the call and is always in the right place at the right time. The new you is blessed and is a blessing, for the grace of God sustains it in every way.

How thankful we are to be so blessed. We arise now to our greatest yet to be, realizing there is nothing to fear. We gratefully leave all of our false beliefs behind as we begin our immaculate journey of profound love, a love which is returned to us, over and over again, magnified and overflowing.

Affirmation:

I willingly allow my greatness to emerge! I live and love fearlessly! I am a servant and the Beloved of God!

Teaching Without Preaching

What the healer does is to mentally uncover and reveal the truth of Being, which is that God is in and through every man, and that this Indwelling Presence is already perfect.

Ernest Holmes, *The Science of Mind*

There are sometimes people in our lives whom we love who are very negative in their thinking and acting. We want them to be more positive because we are sure that they would experience more happiness and joy. Basically, we want them to change, thinking that if they would, our life would be better.

What I've discovered is that all our words and fancy ideas won't change them until they are ready to change, which may be never. Then and only then will they be able to hear. In the meantime, in addition to irritating them, we only bring pain and suffering upon ourselves in our failed attempts. It is not our job to change anyone, though many of us think it is.

When we stand centered in the absolute power and love that is our divine nature, however, being willing to release all judgment towards the one before us, we discover a powerful way to elicit more truth and beauty in whomever or whatever we behold. In that place of centeredness, those who are ready to change will find us.

So we turn within and put our attention on our own process, deepening in our own love, truth and awareness. We then become the perfect point of inspiration, not by what we say but, more powerfully, by how we live our lives. We inspire by loving the ones we are with, recognizing and being compassionate over their sense of powerlessness, rather than judging their negativity. We see beyond their sense of limitation. We do for ourselves what they cannot do and hence become a true example of the principles in action. We always bring the inner work back into our own backyard, not looking to others to make us feel good or using others as an excuse to stay stuck in our own smallness. We teach by example. As Jesus said we become the way, the truth and the life!

Affirmation:

I witness the perfection of all life! I release judgment and my need to fix anyone! I rest in pure compassion, peace and love!

Authentic Power

Humbleness, forgiveness, clarity and love are the dynamics of freedom. They are the foundations of authentic power.

Gary Zukav, *The Seat of the Soul*

The greatest good that can come to anyone is the forming within him of an absolute certainty of himself, and of his relationship to the universe, forever removing the sense of heaven as being outside of himself.

Ernest Holmes, *The Science of Mind*

As I stand in perfect self-acceptance, the need for my ego to announce itself lessens, for my fear of not being loved diminishes. There in my humbleness, my supply is from an internal source, and it is infinite and unconditional and not dependent upon any outer appearance.

With forgiveness, I access the depth of my love, which is infinite and unconditional in its nature. With forgiveness, I cease to project my unhealed self onto the world around me, and I am no longer held captive by my own negative energy. With forgiveness, my mind and heart are set free to see only God before me.

With clarity, I am free from the haze and dust of my own confused thinking. I am clean and pure in my thought. I am easily heard and easily seen. I am free from doubt and guilt. I am unhampered, unqualified, and absolute in my discernment. I am free from entanglement. I am innocent.

With love as my true essence, I project only love in my outer world. That love becomes a healing balm upon the planet. I am set free to be my authentic self. In that freedom lies my true power. It doesn't matter how others see me because I see myself, and I truly love and appreciate what I see.

Affirmation:

I willingly give up my need to control my life. I release myself from false ideas about myself. I see myself as I truly am. I stand boldly in the power of my authentic self.

Liberation

Divine Consciousness is at once creating and manifesting all things and acting in and as all things in various stages of self-disguise.

Andrew Harvey, *The Direct Path*

The sooner we release our minds from the thought that we have to create, the sooner we shall be able to work in line with Spirit.

Ernest Holmes, *The Science of Mind*

Sometimes we think that the harder we struggle, the more successful or affluent we will be, but I have come to see that the struggle is not necessary. In fact, the struggle takes energy that we could use in achieving what we desire in other ways. How can letting go of the struggle bring the very thing one yearns for?

The truth is that the more I let go of my earthly desires and desire only love—to give it and receive it—the more I am in the abundant flow of the universe. My good flows to me from everywhere in surprising ways and more abundantly than I could imagine. My desires are known and fulfilled beyond my expectations. I see that I live in a benevolent, giving universe. What is true is that we all do. It is important that we recognize this so that we can stop doing things in our unconscious humanness that would interrupt the universal flow. We can, and frequently do, unconsciously alter the giving nature of the universe through our faulty thinking.

It is for us to realize that as we begin to take care of God's business—giving and receiving love—our earthly business is handled. The more we are about the business of loving, the more we see how much time we've wasted on the very unimportant. We must let go and have faith that our needs are known and will be handled. We concentrate instead on being more loving in our lives, on doing our spiritual practices of prayer, meditation, and absorbing ourselves in service and activities that uplift the soul. We do not have to work so hard at living. Our attitudes and beliefs about life create our reality. Our freedom, peace, joy, loving and bliss are all awaiting our surrender.

Affirmation:

I let go of the human struggle. I release myself to my loving—giving it and receiving it. I am in appreciation and gratitude for this benevolent universe. I am in the universal flow.

From Forgiveness to Freedom

An unforgiving spirit is a cancer of the soul.

Why do we need forgiveness? Because every one of us has condemned ourselves. And every one of us has tried to work out of our self-hatred by projecting the responsibility for our problems onto others.

Paul Ferrini, *The 12 Steps of Forgiveness*

Recently I have become aware of the importance of self-forgiveness. We often talk about forgiving others, but now I see how important it is that we also forgive ourselves. I am convinced that we cannot find true freedom and liberation in our human walk until we are able to forgive ourselves for our own condemnation. If we cannot let go of our own blame and shame, how can we do that for anyone else? If we cannot see our own innocence and worthiness, then how can we see it in another?

Sometimes we think that we have forgiven the one who hurt us because we have said the right words, but the process of forgiveness goes quite a bit deeper; it comes from within. Often times the mind, through our words, has forgiven, but the body has not. Those unhealed places inside of us become the source of our projections in the outer world. We project our inner issues onto others and then we judge them. All judgments, whether good or bad, have a negative effect on us, even if it is only in our health. In Matthew 18:21, 22, Peter asks Jesus how many times he must forgive his brother who has sinned against him. Jesus says 70 x 7. We must forgive until there is nothing left inside of us that would harm us or keep us in separation.

Of course, it is not easy to forgive ourselves or others because then we have to take responsibility for our lives and all that we think and feel. It is easier to blame some circumstance or someone else for how our lives are turning out. Many of us would rather be right than happy or at peace.

Self-forgiveness is truly the beginning of the path to peace and to experiencing heaven on earth. Fear constricts the world; forgiveness sets it free!

Affirmation:

I forgive myself for anything harmful ever done to me and for anything harmful I have done to another. I release all judgments of myself or others. I set myself free to flourish and prosper.

Disaster Relief

Life from the Center is a life of unhurried peace and power. It is simple. It is serene... And it makes our life programs new and overcoming. We need not get frantic. God is at the helm. And when our little day is done we lie down quietly in peace, for all is well.

Thomas Kelly, *A Testament of Devotion*

How often we try to solve our problems with the same anxiety and stress that got us into them in the first place. We try to solve our problems (and they can truly seem quite big) at the level of the problem. In those moments, our minds are so filled with chatter that there is no way we can hear our own Inner Voice.

If we could hear it, it would be comforting us, assuring us that all is well despite any appearances to the contrary. It would be assuring us that we have everything we need to solve any issue before us, and that we have resources that we have barely tapped. It would be reassuring us that this is a brand new day, a brand new beginning, and that we don't have to continue spinning in circles, getting nowhere fast. It would assure us of the unlimited possibility of our lives and that if we could just be still long enough, in perfect faith and trust, the inspiration and solution to everything would come. It would assure us of our own inherent well being, of our loving and giving nature, and of our innate ability to see truth and live it. It would remind us that we are not alone, and that we live in a world that works for everyone if we can but see it.

We do have a power and a strength within that can handle any seeming difficulty, but first we must become quiet and still. As we listen, a great peacefulness comes over us. We hear the beating of our own heart, and we have a sense that our silent prayer has been answered. Truly all is well… all is well.

Affirmation:

I rest in the assurance of God's infinite love as me. All my needs are met for I am the Beloved of God. I quiet my mind and listen… peace prevails over all!

Restoration

The light of the body is the eye: if therefore thine eye be single,
thy whole body shall be full of light.

Holy Bible, St. Matthew 6:22

There they were, upsetting everything and everyone. They were lying, disrespectful, and taking advantage. They were unconscious and doing whatever they could to survive... at someone else's expense I might add. My friend was crying. It made me furious inside—their disrespect and lack of caring for anybody else's feelings or situation. I saw them as losers. I felt my body tense and, at that moment, my own inner turmoil began. I hated the thought of having to interact with them. I could not see anything of value there. I could feel the anger and upset about their behavior towards my friend rising up inside of me.

But then, something happened. I became aware of my own suffering, and I realized that I was inflicting it upon myself. They had done nothing to me. I began to pray for peace in my heart, for a sense of the love that is my inherent nature. I could feel my body relax, the pain of separation slowly dissipating. I could feel peace coming over me, and I began to ask God over and over again for the right words to say, the right way to show up. It worked. Finally, I could feel nothing but love. I was free. My anguish was over! I knew I would be able to show up as love, and I would know what to say. Light seemed to flood over me. In that instant, I became a beneficial presence in what otherwise might have been a volatile situation.

This is the nature of my work. It is moment by moment, hour by hour, day by day, forever...seeing as God sees; loving as God loves, even when it would seem so much easier to judge and hate and separate myself from the ones who disgust me and whom I feel are undeserving. No one is undeserving of my love which is, in truth, God's love. In my remembrance of that, I realize and will never forget, I am truly set free.

Affirmation:

I remember who I am as Divine Being. I shall love as if my eternal freedom depended upon it.

Return to Love

Light within, thou light divine,
Thou shalt never cease to shine;
Thou canst not depart from me;
We are one, for I am thee.
Darkness flies and sins depart,
Truth is reigning in my heart;
Endless day dispersed the night
When I found I was the Light.

Christian D. Larson, *The Pathway of Roses*

I've been thinking about oneness lately and what that really implies. If it is true that the one before me who has hurt me is really me, then how can I possibly cast a stone at him? It softens my heart to think that he is really the suffering (or angry or violent) part of me that has not quite yet realized its inseparability from God. Why else would he be in my path and in front of me? He would be doing the dance (of love or fire) with someone else. How that eases my heart and enables me then to touch the place of forgiveness inside of me. It is like a fast track to keeping my heart open and my love so present.

I am so appreciative of being able to grasp my connection to all that is at such a deep level. My only job (no matter what confronts me) is to keep my heart open and my love flowing. It is a gift to the one before me and, of course because we are so connected, it is the greatest gift to me! The more I realize the truth of this and the more I practice remembering it in the moment of occurrence, the more my personal suffering diminishes. Ah, it is only that fear-filled part of me that I see before me!

Once again, we are ultimately left to our own devices to create the world of peace and love that we wish to inhabit. We will continue to bump into those who are carrying the message of our own redemption. They show us what we have yet to embrace about ourselves. So I continue to learn and grow, and I remain fearless as I head downstream. I am in the flow. I do not fight with what is. There is a tremendous sense of freedom in that, and I am so grateful!

Affirmation:

I see and embrace my oneness with all of life! I and my brother are one! I forgive him for he is me!

Change is Gonna Come!

You are becoming a conscious spiritual midwife to the next stage of your evolution and to the evolution of love on the planet.

Michael Bernard Beckwith

Rise up, Beloveds! Change is coming! In each and every moment, you are becoming. What you are becoming is your choice and your choice alone. Your life experience is not up to someone else. It is up to you.

This may seem like a big responsibility and some of us would perhaps like to turn it over to someone else rather than take personal responsibility; but whether you are conscious of it or not, your life is in your hands. You can make it glorious or you can make it Hell on earth.

It's time to stop blaming someone else for why our life isn't working. It's time to let go of our self-destructive patterns and wake up to who we truly are as powerful, creative geniuses. We cannot continue to hide out and deny our power and perfection. It is time to step into our greatness in a whole new way—unafraid to be seen and heard or to reveal who we truly are. We are a creation of God! How can that not be good enough? How can we deny the world the opportunity to meet and savor the wisdom, joy, love, compassion and peace that is our true essence? The truth is our life is not determined by our history. It is determined by the choices we make in each moment. We can change everything by simply making a different choice—a choice that promotes love on the planet.

Are you willing to choose differently? Are you willing to be big for God? I am grateful for I see a new day ahead—a day filled to overflowing with peace, joy and love on the planet. My eye is single upon God!

Affirmation:

I celebrate the freedom from my own self-inflicted bondage! I'm willing to become big enough to receive the blessing I've been asking for!

Self-Taught

You did not come here as teachers in this time to teach everyone, because everyone isn't seeking what you are.

Abraham-Hicks

What a burden is lifted from me when I realize that I am not here to change the world, and the world will change because of me.

What a burden is lifted when I let go of the belief that I have to have all the answers, yet all the answers lie within me.

What a burden is lifted when I let go of the arrogance that I am better than someone else, yet I am perfection itself.

What a burden is lifted when I realize that I can lean into God as my very life and know that who I am speaks louder than any words I could ever utter.

We are here to love the Self of us (capital S) unconditionally. The Self of us is God in the flesh. When we come into complete alignment with the Self of us, there is nothing or no one else to impress. We have met then the Master Teacher Jesus. We are, as a result, truly humbled.

So we look within to take the measure of our own motives and actions in the world. We keep our eye single upon God, and everything works together for our good and for the good of everyone else around us. Our vibration attracts the very ones who are seeking what we have to offer. It is easy and it is effortless.

So I look in the mirror and what do I see? The Self of me, the Presence of God stares back at me. It is my job to love it unconditionally.

Affirmation:

The power and wisdom of God lies within me, and I am humbled and grateful for God's presence as my life!

God's Eyes

Your consciousness which is imbued with truth is the temple of God, and they enter here to receive healing...

Joel S. Goldsmith, *The Foundation of Mysticism*

My inner eye is open; look at what I've become.

Michael Bernard Beckwith

Who is looking through these eyes of mine? Who is living in this body? Who am I? Who am I really?

I do believe that I have transcended the simple answer to that question. I can see beyond seeing. I can see the suffering, yet see something beyond that. I can see a greater truth. I can read the newspaper and recognize a world in conflict and turmoil, yet I see a brighter day. I have come to be a witness to the perfection all around me.

This is a new day. We cannot dwell on or solve the problem at the level of the problem. We have to focus on what we want to see. We have to focus on the beauty and perfection—even on what doesn't seem so perfect humanly. On some level, it is all perfection. In our willingness to behold the perfection, the door opens for more light and love to reveal itself. We are not here to fight against what is. We are here to see the glory of the Lord everywhere. In our ability to see that, the whole world is set free.

At last I have a formula for my own personal success in this world. I behold only God before me, and more God shows up! I cannot fall into the pit of woe-is-me thinking about anything. I stay conscious—so heightened in my awareness that ease and grace meet me everywhere. It's not a Pollyanna existence. Worrying and fear never fixed anything! I am surrendered into a divine idea about my existence and the existence of all those around me. My consciousness goes before me and makes the way smooth. God is seen through me. At last my eyes are open!

Affirmation:

With gratitude, I am able to see as I am seen! Look at what I've become!

Coming Home

Peace be unto thee, stranger, enter and be not afraid.

I have left the gate open and thou art welcome to my home…

Sit and rest and refresh your soul…

All, all is yours, and you are welcome.

Ernest Holmes, *The Science of Mind*

We are constantly expanding into a greater version of ourselves. The problem we face sometimes is that we are not yet up to speed with who and what we have become, so physically we appear to be going through darkness. It can feel very uncomfortable because negative feelings and thoughts arise as though we've gone backwards instead of forwards.

The new idea or dream for your life is born within you and immediately your inner being accepts and moves into that new idea of who you've become. The law of attraction responds to the new you and brings all that you need to you easily and effortlessly. It is a stream of well being. The difficulty is our ability to get out of our own way. We often resist what we have already internally become by our negative thoughts and doubts about ourselves—either hashing over our past failures or asking whether we are enough. Can I really do this life I've dreamed of—can I really be that great? When you resist, you experience the negative emotions. When you don't, you thrive.

If you stay in the present moment and quit resisting (worrying or thinking negative thoughts about the past or future), you will thrive. You inner being will bring you, through the law of attraction, all that you've asked for. Things are supposed to work out for you. It's your job to keep up with your expansion by thinking thoughts that are positive and uplifting.

Make peace with where you are. There is nothing to worry about or fret over. The expanded version of you is always calling, so let go and let the swift current bring you home! All is yours and you are welcome!

Affirmation:

I willingly let go of all resistance and I come joyously home to myself.

Truth to Tell

To serve the human race in the largest and highest sense, we must bring forth into living expression the truest, the best and the greatest that we can possibly find in the depths of our own sublime being.

Christian D. Larson, The Pathway of Roses

Is it service or servitude? The beauty and wonder of our life is that we have or should have dominion over it. In service, we have dominion. In servitude, we do not. Now this is the hard question. Are you in service in your life or servitude?

If, as Jesus tells us, the Kingdom of God is within us, then right where we are there is, at the very least, joy, peace, beauty, abundance, creativity and freedom. The well is full and there is plenty to drink. We give and serve from the overflow. If, on the other hand, one is serving but not from a place of dominion over one's life, then one is in servitude. In servitude, we feel resentful, taken advantage of, irritated, overwhelmed or somehow abused by our circumstances.

As in everything, it is clearly our responsibility to take care of ourselves, to check in with ourselves to see if we are in alignment with our own truth. When we check in with ourselves, we have an opportunity to see where we are coming from. Are we practicing self-love and self-compassion? Are we taking care of our own needs? Do we need to shift our attitude in order to come from a place of love and true service? How can we turn what we perceive as servitude into service? How can we serve from a more joyful heart?

Sometimes it is having a direct conversation to gain clarity and be in alignment with our own inner guidance. Sometimes it's actually being willing and able to say "no." Only you know how to take care of yourself and how to stay in complete integrity with the Self. It is in service, not servitude, that we receive the enormous gift of love beyond compare.

Affirmation:

I nurture and love my God-Self and serve from a wellspring of unconditional love.

The Passion of God

Do you realize that the greatest thing that you can give to the planet is to be happy... you are a cell in the mind of God and when you begin to be happy through the fulfillment of your soul... you begin to affect the other cells around you unconsciously...

Michael Bernard Beckwith

The passion of God is infinite love. It is not doing what you think you should out of fear or the possibility of receiving some outward approval, but rather the happiness that comes forth when one truly falls in love with the Christ Presence within. The pathway is opened up then for great works as an everyday experience. We cannot measure the impact we have in the world as one who is inseparable from the eternal source of all life. The gateway is open then to receive all the blessings of God and to be the joyous blessing that others have been waiting for.

The difficulty for most of us in this physical experience is resisting the impulse to limit ourselves by setting our own boundaries beyond which we think we cannot go. We do this all the time by the words we speak about ourselves, our expectations of the possibility for our lives and the limited way in which we see ourselves. Actually, there are no limits—only those we establish for ourselves. The source of

God is endless supply. You are free to be as big as you want to be, or as small. It is all up to you. When the blinders come off, ultimately we see that we are creating our universe and everything in it.

The power lies within you to create the life of your dreams, but all the preparation takes place in the silence of your own soul. You will not get it in a book or from your guru. It is peeling away, layer by layer, your own self-inflicted thought forms to create paradise on earth.

The journey is worth it. The greatest lover you have ever known awaits you. Blessings be to those who radiate the joy and love of God!

Affirmation:

I joyfully answer my soul's call! I open up to a new idea of myself! I am sourced in all ways from the wellspring of God's love!

Divine Union

Love is at the center of man's being, and the calm, continuous pulsations of life are governed by love.

Ernest Holmes, *The Science of Mind*

Keep thy heart with all diligence, for out of it are the issues.

Holy Bible, Proverbs 4:23

During my first trip to Egypt, I had an experience of the deep and powerful unconditional love that resides in the midst of me. It lasted only a short while—fleeting in terms of a lifetime—but it was so profound, I shall never forget it. It was what I called later a Jesus moment as I walked around embracing and loving everyone near me. I was in a state of bliss and the giving of the love was the receiving of the love. There was no difference for I had become the love.

The love that I describe is in the midst of every one of us. It is our true nature. So much of the time, however, our love is really quite conditional, even with the ones closest to us. We love them if they do what we say, agree with us, or fulfill our needs in some way. We can turn off the love, though, just like a faucet if they disappoint us. Often times, we choose to argue our point and be "right" rather than to be love. We choose separation.

I have come to see that if we don't love ourselves, our ability to love others is limited and qualified. We project onto others those unlovable aspects of ourselves that we have not made peace with. We love others, expecting something in return. The more we come into full acceptance of ourselves and begin to love every aspect of who we are, the richer our relationships will be with others. We begin to love not from a place of need, but from a place of peace and contentment. Then we experience the giving and receiving of love as inseparable. Finally, we have found the love we've been seeking, and discover that it has been here all the time!

Affirmation:

I open my heart and allow my love to expand. I let go of judgment and my need to be right. I dive deep into the well of unconditional love.

Let Me Reveal Myself

The greatest good that can come to anyone is the forming within him of an absolute certainty of himself, and of his relationship to the universe, forever removing the sense of heaven as being outside of himself.

Ernest Holmes, *The Science of Mind*

Sometimes we carry the burden of a past so thick with shame and remorse, that we think no one could possibly love us if they knew the truth about us. We are imprisoned in a sense by our guilt and shame. Outwardly we carry ourselves as if everything is alright. It seems like a great masquerade. We say to ourselves, if they only knew the truth about me, I would never be accepted by them.

The truth of the matter is that our story is rarely so unique that it hasn't been heard a hundred times before. The truth is that you are not your story, no matter how awful it seems to you and how much you feel it marks you for life. The rich fiber of your being is perfection and wholeness. We often project the guilt and shame of another onto ourselves, or we make some very bad choices before we know better. We are not bound forever by our history. We can consider it part of our learning that turns us into the understanding, compassionate person we have become today. In other words, hard to believe, but perhaps it was all a gift. Your excuse for poor living is gone. You have no excuse. The choice for great living is yours to make. The question becomes are you going to make that choice or continue to bemoan your fate until the end of your time on the planet?

Let me reveal myself—the truth of me as the divine emanation of God. I release my story—my faulty thinking—my unbelief. I am enraptured by the great God who loves me so unconditionally! I am enraptured and filled to overflowing with God's love!

Affirmation:

I release any idea of myself as less than perfect! I accept the truth of my divine and holy nature! I rest in God!

On Becoming!

Real bliss and ecstasy come from activating one's potential, not mere accomplishment or getting things. The real message behind that is, on the way to accomplishment, you have to become something.

Michael Bernard Beckwith

Unity Magazine, September/October 2007

I have asked myself sometimes, "Where am I going?" as though that were the important question. Yet my life—this outstanding joy-filled journey that I'm on—seems so present, so purposeful, so life-affirming, so powerfully good and filled with so many blessings. Everything seems so perfect and so right in my world. Yet sometimes I ask myself, "Where am I going? What am I supposed to be doing?" as though I'm not doing it now.

And then I remind myself that I'm already doing it. I'm becoming. It isn't about my destination. I'm living the fullness of my God-life right now. I'm joyously in the giving and receiving of life. I'm loving myself more and opening my heart to others in a more profound way. I'm seeing more clearly and listening to others more acutely. I'm loving and sharing of myself and my goods more generously. My barriers are down, and love is flooding in and out of me. I have grown comfortable living in the unknown, being unattached to outcomes, knowing that I'm always guided and directed. I listen inwardly and follow that inner guidance and because of that, I find myself in the right place at the right time. I know that my good will come to me. I need not struggle for it. I remain open and ready to receive.

I'm becoming! Thank God I'm becoming! There is nothing to worry about. My life is blessed. If I die tomorrow, the important thing is that I have joyously lived today!

Affirmation:

I celebrate my life as the life of God! I'm becoming more aware of my true identity! I can rest in the assurance that everything I need is already here! I'm becoming!

Seeds of Love

Love is like a soft, warm light, warming the heart and glowing in every atom of being, radiating out into the farthest corners of our experience.

Jack Addington

Sometimes we get so caught up in our negative thinking that we forget all about that which brings us such joy. We forget who we are and all the opportunities we have to express our complete joy. Then we read something or have a loving encounter which reminds us of all that is joyful and wonder-filled in our lives and once again, we experience heaven on earth.

Heaven is here now—frankly you can change your mind instantly and begin to see the beauty and love everywhere. You can recapture the moments of ecstatic living that have so enriched your life. You can begin to savor all the splendid times when you had a complete sense of well being even when there was nothing in particular that made a day special. For me, it can be recalling the smell of new mown grass on a warm summer evening or the smell of something delicious cooking for me or the times of laughter and joy on an outing with a good friend or lover.

How quickly our minds can change from fear and hopelessness to peace and beauty unbounded—the tension of worry gone in an instant replaced with a sense of gratitude and well being. Seeds of love have been planted everywhere. Only good comes to us when we are focusing in gratitude on the good that has been planted throughout time in receptive, fertile soil.

Your joy and freedom are only a thought away. Love abounds for you and around you. The seeds have already been planted; and if you choose, you can step into heaven on earth right now!

Affirmation:

I remember all that is beautiful and loving in my life! I cultivate thoughts that enrich my existence! My garden is planted with seeds of love!

See Rightly

For with thee is the fountain of life; in thy light shall we see light.

Holy Bible, Psalm 36:9

How easy it would be to get caught up in the negative economic news as reported by the media. My friend owns a bead store in a suburban community in New Jersey. All around her, stores are closing down. Yet there she sits in the middle of seeming chaos, her store bustling with activity and energy. My friend realized long ago that her life and her store are ministries of good will and revelation and that she is sourced by the creator of all things. It is such a testimony of her consciousness. She is in the world but not of it.

This is our challenge—to see beyond seeing, to know a greater truth. We live above the fray; and because we do, we can see so much clearer and make decisions that are for the good of all concerned rather than from a fear of lack and limitation.

We can begin to live from a greater knowing that we are sustained in a loving, giving universe that supplies all of our needs. We can draw a distinction between falsehood and reality. In consciousness, we create our experience. It takes discernment and discipline to keep our thoughts on that which is greater. Infinite wisdom directs us.

Whatever we ought to know, we know; and whatever we ought to do, we do, all with the awareness that whatever belongs to us will come to us easily and effortlessly.

Our lives shall be fulfilled for that is the promise of the Kingdom. Divine Intelligence molds our every thought and decision, which then manifests as our experience, and we are set free to live the life of our dreams.

How wonderful to be alive in this time of great creativity and to know that freedom, prosperity and joy are ours today!

Affirmation:

I take dominion over my life today! I see the perfection of life all around me! I receive the infinite bounty of the universe!

Feel Free!

Feel Free!...You know you want to!

Theresa Walker from her CD *"The Next Big Thing"*

There is a wonderful song that makes me feel like dancing. When Theresa sings "Feel free, dirty your dress... you know you want to," I think immediately of the word "naughty." From the beginning of our journey on the planet, we have been conditioned to stay "in the box." If Mom said to hang up my dress and I did so, I was a good girl—I was nice. I was staying inside the box of acceptable behavior. If not, I was outside the box and naughty. If a teacher laid down rules and I followed them, I was in the box and nice—a good girl. If not, I was outside the box and naughty. This conditioning goes on and on throughout our adult years.

This song is inviting us to be free and play outside the box. Heaven on earth cannot be found in the box. The outer world has nothing for us of a lasting nature, yet we do what is commonly accepted in the external world as dictated by someone other than ourselves. We let ourselves and our lives be ruled by outside opinions and influences.

Songwriter Theresa Walker and I are inviting you to step outside the box. All the great ones have—Jesus the Christ, Martin Luther King,

Gandhi, and many others. The seed of genius is within you. We are here to offer our gifts. It will require the courage to step out of the box, to come out from among them, to be in the world but not of it. But the payoff is delicious! It is an opportunity to finally dance your dance and sing the song you came here to sing. No one can sing your song as wonderfully as you can. The world is waiting. The music is playing... so sing, beautiful one, sing!

Affirmation:

I am an individualized expression of the One! I contain all the attributes of Supreme Being! I am powerful beyond measure! My life is the life of God!

Resurrected Once Again

The resurrection is the death of the belief that we are separated from God. For death is to the illusion alone and not to Reality. God did not die. What happened was that man awoke to Life.

Ernest Holmes, *The Science of Mind*

The love within you is greater than any loss, any diagnosis, and greater than death itself. How many times have I died only to be born again out of the ashes of my disbelief. How many times has my precious God loved me through the tempests of my own doubt, fear and feelings of unworthiness.

Yes, here I am cleansed and standing once again at the beginning of my life—more powerful, more loving, more giving, more aware of who I am and more aligned with the truth of my being. Here I am resurrected once again.

This is the story of our human incarnation on the planet. We continue to die daily and to be reborn again. Surprisingly, yes there is more to forgive, more to embrace about our own humanity and the humanity of our brothers and sisters who have chosen to walk with us, and always, always more love to express as it expands from the center of our being.

Our human incarnation is a holy walk when we choose to see it as such. It is a deliverance from the fears and doubts that may plague us in the beginning but which cannot withstand the onslaught of the all-encompassing love of God.

How grateful I am for my divine walk. How grateful I am for the love-beauty which has taken over my life. How grateful I am that throughout all of it, I have been so loved, so guided and so cared for. This is the promise for those who are courageous enough to stay the course. The expanded love you embrace with each resurrection never dies, and you are in love for the rest of your life. That is your Divine inheritance!

Affirmation:

Gratitude, focus and high resolve birth transformation in my life! Every day I become a better version of my true self! I am constantly evolving into all that God created me to be!

The Divine Mother

He who loves me in whatever he sees, wherever this man may live, in truth, he lives in me.

Bhagavad Gita

Whether or not you had a wonderful, loving mother during this physical incarnation, it is not too late to experience great mothering. We can be to ourselves the great mother we never had. In fact, it is a wonderful way to become that loving presence to everyone we meet as we begin to express that love to the one before us in the mirror.

If we only knew how much God loves us, we would never hurt ourselves in the way we do. We would look with such loving eyes in the mirror and see before us the splendid, unique, perfect creation of God—so worthy of love, so worthy to know joy and freedom, so worthy of receiving all the gifts that heaven on earth promises to us. We would love ourselves unconditionally and never compare ourselves to another, finding ourselves falling short. We would never judge ourselves harshly nor question why we were born.

We would see in the mirror just what the most loving mother sees when she beholds her beloved child. We would embrace ourselves with loving arms. We would love unconditionally. We would see the love-beauty in the radiance of our face. We would behold the perfection and wholeness of pure Spirit. We would see as God sees, and we would begin to live from that place. Then what a blessing we would be as we walk in the world, able to also see the perfection in our brothers and sisters. We would see beauty no matter what the appearance. We would see love. We would see from the perspective of the Divine Mother.

It is not too late. You can begin today. Love yourself. Nurture yourself. Mother yourself and take time every day for a private appointment with the Divine Mother within your own soul.

Affirmation:

Today I bathe myself in the unconditional, comforting love of the Divine Mother. I choose to keep my heart open and fall in love again and again and again... then I shall see perfection. I shall see God!

My Spiritual Father

Fear not, little flock; for it is your Father's good pleasure to give you the kingdom.

Holy Bible, Luke 12:32

It doesn't matter whether we felt loved, cared for and protected by our human, earthly father; our Beloved Spiritual father has loved us forever unconditionally. Whether we were listening or not, our Father has been guiding and directing us since the beginning of time.

When we surrender and are willing to have faith and trust in what we cannot see, miracles are made manifest. We are supported in a universe that is working together for our good. We cannot fail because there is no failure in God. We only have to say "yes" to Divine Spirit to experience the perfect orchestration that is a life devoted to God. Beauty is all around us. The love and support we need shows up in many guises. We are supplied by that which is limitless. We are in the right place doing the right thing. Nothing but gratitude illumines our awareness for we have been set free from the worries of the third dimensional world. What is for us finds us in the most perfect way. And one knows then the intensity and preciousness of God's love for Its beloved. One begins to experience heaven on earth in one's daily walk.

How do we claim this inheritance as our own? We release resistance, open up and expand the heart space while truly yielding to the ineffable, supreme lover of all life—God.

How wonderful to call myself a servant of God for God is love and I am then a servant of love. I humbly give praise and thanksgiving to my Spiritual Father, my Papa.

Affirmation:

My life is a perfect expression of Divine Spirit! The God in me sees the God in you! I am free to be the me I came to be!

Free-falling with God

Observe the ravens; for they do not sow or reap, and they have no storerooms and barns; and yet God feeds them; how much more important are you than the birds?

Holy Bible, Lamsa Translation, Luke 12:24

From June of 2009 to October of 2013, I was the Spiritual Director of the Symphony of Life Spiritual Center in Ojai, California. This was never my plan. In fact, I don't remember ever saying that I wanted to be the minister of a church, and my life took so many miraculous twists and turns to get to that place. Yet I know that I was in the right place doing the right thing.

The free-fall has to do with surrender, faith and trust. The free-fall has to do with saying "yes" to Divine guidance. The free-fall has to do with continuing to remember the sweet words "I will never leave you nor forsake you." (Hebrews 13:5) God loves us so much, and that part of us, our higher Self (the God within) knows exactly how to get us where we are supposed to be if we but listen. We do need to cast off our fear and resistance, though, and our need to control— the thought that we can do it better from our little personality mind. If we can think it, it's not big enough.

So I continue to surrender, bathing in the sweetness of God's enduring love. I lean into that which has carried me to places I never dreamed I would go. I am in service to the higher calling of my soul. It is a most glorious time to be this much in love with life and to have this much joy in my heart. The peace comes instantly when I remember who sent me and who loves me beyond measure. The peace comes instantly when I remember that I'm just an instrument of the Divine and I don't have to make the music alone.

Affirmation:

I allow God to express through me in the most miraculous way! I rest in the sweetness of God's enduring love!

I Love You Again

Behold what manner of love the Father hath bestowed upon us, that we should be called the sons of God...

Holy Bible, 1 John 3:1

If you have believed in an illusion that has kept you stuck in life— some of us for our whole life   now is the time to forgive ourselves and the other. Now is the time to love again and for the very first time. When we let go of the illusion we've been living under, we can begin again. We can free ourselves from the mistaken idea we had about who we are and about our brothers and sisters on the planet. We were certain they were going to take care of us and provide all that we needed. We were relying on them instead of the Infinite Source of All Good—God. The illusion was of our own creation. Now we are willing to see it for what it was, and let it go! Until we let it go, we are held captive by our own faulty thinking. We are imprisoned by our own thoughts.

I forgive myself for believing in the illusion. I forgive myself for the illusion I created about my brothers and sisters and what they had to do to please me. I love again and for the first time. Everything else you've been praying for comes with ease and grace once you can forgive yourself and your brothers and sisters. This forgiveness is what releases the good to flow again in your direction. This is God's promise. Love is the way.

Affirmation:

I love you again and for the first time.

Living in the Absolute

...all power is given unto me in heaven and in earth.

Holy Bible, Matthew 28:18

I could choose to stay small and believe that I live in a world filled with suffering and pain, but I have chosen instead to become consciously aware of the Divine Presence and the Divine Power, the wholeness of Truth, of Love, of Wisdom—the eternal Good which is my nature. I have chosen God and life everlasting. I have chosen goodness and mercy. I have chosen to be forgiving and loving in my heart. I have chosen to be present with myself and others in each and every moment. I have chosen peace over anger and warfare. I have chosen light over darkness and an inner knowing that my needs will be fulfilled by the Infinite Source of all supply.

As I stand resolute in my knowing of God as my life, divine harmony and peace flow in and through me. Beauty is everywhere. My eyes can see the blessings. I see beyond the illusion of fear and separation. My life is filled with happiness, good health and joy. I commune daily with the Invisible Presence which peoples the world with the manifestation of Its Life, Its Light and Its Love.

It is from this place that the miracles begin to happen—the perfect persons, situations, and experiences come into my life. I am guided onto a path that leads me to where I'm supposed to be. I am in the right place doing the right thing. The universe is working on my behalf.

I joyfully surrender in perfect faith and trust. My life is filled with grace. I am the Beloved. I see it now. I am living in the absolute. I am set free. My heart overflows with gratitude!

Affirmation:

I live in the absolute! God is my source and supply! I know that Good alone has power in my life!

In Appreciation

Yea, the Lord shall give that which is good, and our land shall yield her increase.

Holy Bible, Psalm 85:12

When I appreciate, I'm in a divine activity that carries me into such a state of grace, well-being and harmony that no words are necessary and no negative thoughts can penetrate. I can choose to elevate my vibration through appreciation at any time, and it becomes a spiritual practice. I can decide at any moment to focus on all the wonderful aspects in my life and place my attention completely there.

The other day, the power in our house was out for a whole day. It never occurred to me how many areas of my life would be affected by a loss of power. When the power came back on at 8:00 p.m. that night, I felt such appreciation for all the things I take for granted, and such gratitude for all that I have. I felt enormous gratitude and thanksgiving for the very basic conveniences of life.

There are so many things we can appreciate about our lives. As we move into the activity of appreciation, we dance in the realm of the Infinite. Our vibration is high, more good enters our awareness and our life manifests accordingly.

What do we value, prize, treasure and cherish? There's enough there to keep us busy in the activity of appreciation all day every day. In this human incarnation, we are given the freedom to create heaven on earth. We can live there most of the time by making the choice to be in constant praise and thanksgiving as a spiritual practice. As the high vibration of appreciation flows out from us, we correspondingly bring goodness, well-being and healing to the planet.

Affirmation:

I appreciate all that I have and am grateful for it! I welcome the God good that flows into my life!

Making Peace with What Is

...in every thing by prayer and supplication with thanksgiving let your requests be made known unto God; and the peace of God, which passeth all understanding, shall keep your hearts and minds through Christ Jesus.

Holy Bible, Philippians 4:6-7

The war inside of us is over the minute we let go of our resistance to what is. We cannot change what is. We can only change what we think about it.

Many people have great difficulty with holidays. They may be facing circumstances or situations that are less than ideal. The holidays are often filled with emotional turmoil, but we have the capacity to create any experience we want to have.

What you fight against persists, but what if you do it differently this time? What if you let go of resistance and accept what is before you? What if you cease to judge it, but instead make peace with it?

We are not here to change the world, but the world will change because we are in it. You can create your own holiday experience. You don't have to do it the way you've always done it in the past. You can do it differently this time and focus on what is great about that particular time of year… the generosity and cheerful air of those around you… the warmth of loving exchanges and well wishes… the music and songs of love and peace. Yes, joy can be your template. You have a choice. You can choose to be filled with gratitude and thanksgiving for all you have to be grateful for. You can choose to be a place of peace, love and joy. You can create the best holiday you've ever had.

When we make peace with what is, we are free then to create something entirely new. We open ourselves to receive the true gifts of every holiday season. We see the perfection all around us and are glorified in God.

Affirmation:

In peace and love, I open myself to receive God's blessings! I rejoice in my ability to choose the light!

Divine Flow

It is the centre where we find that we both receive from all and flow out to all.

Thomas Troward

Love is our highest word and the synonym for God.

Emerson

I've had the realization that for most of my life, my love spigot was half open—that is, the measure of my love was at half flow. During that time, I've been married, raised a child, and have met and befriended many people. Yet I realize that I could have loved more. A dear friend of mine recently assured me, however, that the love I had to give then was probably great enough, but feels like a half measure compared to the love I'm now experiencing as my life.

The love available to us to give and receive is infinite. I know now that it is immeasurable; and if we continue our journey with openness and a willingness to know ourselves completely as God created us, the love continues to expand. There is no limit to the love within us.

It is a profound realization to look back on my life and see in every instance how much more I could have loved. This is not to beat myself up; I no longer do that. It is rather an opportunity to realize and appreciate who I've become. I'm so grateful to know this love as myself and to now deliver my life from a wide-open spigot! It is a blessing to open up to God as Love in this way. I am sure that there is more yet to come. It is powerful living.

I shall not be afraid to love from the fullness of who I am as God, fully expressed as the Beloved in flesh.

Affirmation:

I continue to open myself to greater love. I am free and fearless in my living and loving.

Divine Perfect Being

Spiritual progress is when one becomes free not only of the knowledge which is inevitably from the past, but also from the need to know.

Ravi Ravindra, *The Quest*

"As the Buddha said, all beings are given ten thousand joys and ten thousand sorrows. People we love will die, some dreams will come true, and some will not. Some things we hold as precious will get broken. It is our inevitable inheritance in a human life. It is not about us; it is not something we need take personally." (Ravindra)

We will experience pain, but it is our choice how much we suffer. If we did not want to experience the ups and downs and the ins and outs of life, we would not have entered these physical bodies. It is true exhilaration to live full out, understanding along the way that there will be good times and bad.

As we develop our spiritual practices and our skills at self mastery, we find, however, that we experience fewer times of pain and suffering and more love and joy as we become conscious creators of all that is grand and glorious. We listen and become tuned into the inner language of the soul. We begin to see that we are not victims of anything, that we have the power to change and create a whole new experience more in alignment with our true nature and purpose for being.

As we have been told so many times before, we are beautiful, amazing, perfect creations of God, no less than the roses and lilies. We did not come here to suffer; we came to experience the joy and delight of full-out living. As we are willing to surrender our small thinking mind, we access Infinite Mind, and we see the oneness of all life. We finally see that we are part of the Infinite which is everything and everywhere.

Affirmation:

In peace and love, I listen to the inner voice, in trust and faith that I am the Beloved. Everything is working together for my good.

Being Present With the Presence

Past and future veil God from our sight; burn up both of them with fire.

Rumi

I'm learning how to live in joy most of the time. I'm watching my thoughts. If I'm not present in this moment, I'm either thinking about the past or living in the future. When I feel anxious, uneasy, stressed or worried—all forms of fear—I know that I have slipped into thinking about something in the future, and the future is all an illusion.

When I feel regretful, guilty, have some grievance or resentment or feel sad, I find that I have slipped into the past. In the present moment, there is only the freedom of peace and love beauty. I see that I have no problems. In that moment, I'm now living in a state of consciousness free from all negativity.

We can control our experience. Sometimes we have an issue that is causing so much concern. We feel we have to solve it with our minds. The problems of the mind cannot be solved on the level of the mind. When you move into the present, your problems solve themselves. When you are present with the Presence, you have access to Infinite Intelligence. You move into the light and whatever is exposed to the light itself becomes light. It's the only place where true change can occur and where the past can be dissolved.

Being in the present moment releases me from pain and suffering and frees me from my egoic mind. I experience the love, joy and peace of God, all states of Being which have no opposite. My world has become more intensely beautiful. We prove everything by our living of it. All doubts fall away and only pure loving remains. I am safe and secure in a loving world.

Affirmation:

My peace lies in present moment awareness. Love is my state of Being. I am free.

The Inward Journey

In order for the deepest things in us to be touched and kindled, both fear and anxiety must be wiped away. The one thing that they cannot abide is conscious exposure to the Love of God.

Howard Thurman, *For the Inward Journey*

In one lifetime, I've lived many lives. It is as though in each case, it was a different person doing the living. What is reassuring to me about that is the fact that we are all evolving not of the Spirit, which is already Perfect, but of the mind which so often is blindly groping in the dark.

We are doing the best we can with the limited information we have at the time. Living is an art. We look at the outside world, so sure in our minds that the problem is "out there." Then, before we know it, we are forced to look inside to see that the problems or circumstances we face are not external. They are within. It's not about someone else changing or fixing what's wrong, or changing our outer world so that we can be happy. It's about us waking up to the illusion we've been living under, coming out of our ignorance to see the light of day. Oh, I say—I should be more loving in my heart. I should be more forgiving and nonjudgmental. I did not realize how I had been shutting myself off from the ones that I professed to love.

So this continued deepening happens within, and suddenly I discover that I live in a more loving world. The whole world changes around me because I have changed. I'm happier! I'm more joyful! I'm surprised that there was even more love in me to give. I see that we will never come to the end of our capacity to love.

Each new season brings another opportunity to expand the love within me, and I am forever grateful.

Affirmation:

I shall be expanding forever into a greater version of Divine Love! My joy is unbounded!

Love Note

Just sit there right now. Don't do a thing. Just rest. For your separation from God is the hardest work in this world.

Hafiz

I must tell you about my lover. In the presence of this One, I am never doubtful or fearful. My heart expands in the mere contemplation of how easy and beautiful life is. Somehow I see with new eyes that measure everything with compassion and acceptance. As I am open and receptive, miracles happen every day. I used to call them coincidences.

This Beloved of mine wants only joy and happiness for me. It stands by me during my most challenging times and gives me strength and answers my non-stop questions about life and love. I trust my lover's wisdom for it has never let me down.

In the presence of this One, I grow more loving and more forgiving every day. I want to give to others that same sense of safety and security It gives to me. It doesn't matter how hurt, betrayed or disappointed we have been in the past, a new life awaits us with the willingness to open up to this great lover. It is a complete love. Nothing is missing. It seems so simple compared to the ways I've tried to love in the past. This time, I seek nothing, for everything I need is already here. I have no desire to change anything.

This Beloved demands nothing from me. When I am afflicted by conditions in my human life, I simply ask and my Beloved is immediately present to minister to my every wound. I am so grateful to know the depth of this loving, to realize that the fullness of It is within me, that the more I love, the freer I become.

Joyfully, I have awakened from the sleep of believing we have been apart.

Affirmation:

As God's Beloved, I am never alone. In sickness and health, it is my lover's great pleasure to love me!

Imagination

I am imagination. I can see what the eyes cannot see. I can hear what the ears cannot hear. I can feel what the heart cannot feel.

Peter Nivio Zarlenga

I have recently become so aware of the importance of holding in our thoughts the highest ideals and desires for ourselves. Albert Einstein said imagination is everything. It is the preview of life's coming attractions.

Our will and our imagination are two natural human powers for altering reality. Ernest Holmes tells us that will power may be necessary as a directive agency, but as a creative agency, it is non-existent. It is our imagination that is the creative power. When the imagination creates an image and the will directs and uses that image, miracles happen. The imagination must precede the will in order to produce the greatest possible effect.

So we dream! We dream of the life we desire. We hold in our thoughts that which we want to see manifest. We build in consciousness what we desire to see in form. We cannot underestimate the creative power of our minds. Every great advance in science has come from someone's audacity of imagination.

This ever-changing world we are currently living in needs thinkers now who are bold enough to think "outside the box." That means using our imagination and allowing it to carry us into infinite possibility. All that is now proven was once imagined. The creative genius is within us for there is only One Infinite Mind.

What an excellent life when we let ourselves imagine great things, when we free ourselves from our own self-imposed constraints, when we break the bond with mediocrity and rise to our highest potential! As Norman Cousins once said, "The tragedy of life is not death, but what we let die inside of us while we live."

Affirmation:

I open my mind to the infinite possibilities of life! I see myself joyfully living my dreams!

Independence Day

The Divine Plan is one of Freedom. The inherent nature of man is ever seeking to express itself in terms of freedom, because freedom is the birthright of every living soul.

Ernest Holmes

Your soul yearns for freedom—freedom from the illusions of everyday life, freedom from self-inflicted pain and suffering, freedom from the bondage of negative thought forms, freedom from fear, doubt and worry! Your soul yearns to love fully, to dance and sing and be creative, to be joyful in every waking moment and to live with the awareness of infinite possibility.

Those of us who have gained material goods are locked in fear, doubt and worry about keeping and acquiring more of the goods, and those striving to get material goods are locked in fear, doubt and worry that they won't get the goods. It is all fear, doubt and worry nonetheless than runs our lives. Fear is the driving force in our culture today.

What if love was the driving force? What if our first thought was, "How can I be more loving in my heart?" Love releases all blocks to Divine Sourcing. Once we truly know that God is the source of everything, and it is unlimited, we are free from our need to hoard goods as though there is not enough to go around. We are free then from our own lack and limitation consciousness. When love becomes the driving force, every cell, tissue and organ responds to the Divine Healing taking place in the body temple. When love becomes the driving force, all needs are met easily and effortlessly. When love becomes the driving force, we see our neighbor as ourselves. Yes, when love becomes the driving force, we are truly, truly free at last!

The world needs your love now. Claim your independence! Be willing to have your first thought be, "How can I be more loving in my heart?"

Affirmation:

I rise in God, in love, in wholeness! Love is the driving force in my life! I am fearless in every way for I am sustained and supported in a loving universe!

The Divine Light Within

God said, "I am made whole by your life. Each soul, each soul completes me."

Hafiz

For many of us, it is easy to believe in something outside of ourselves, but not so easy to believe in the one whose face we see when we look in the mirror.

Yet we are told that at core we are spiritual beings—that God works through us, as us. If that is true, then we must behold and love the one whose image we see in the looking glass. I'm not talking about that kind of self-centered adoration of the ego. I'm talking about waking up to the worthiness, the preciousness and lovability of our own sacred Self.

We are imbued with grace and the infinite wisdom of the father of fathers and the mother of mothers. There in the center of us we find a deep resilience of Being. There in the midst of us is the fortitude and strength to hold everything together no matter what's going on in the outer world. In this great knowing, we transcend the small self, the fear-filled self.

We wake up to who we truly are. This takes great surrender in great humility. Finally, we must leave behind any notion that we are not good enough or big enough to step into such a vital and important role. I understand who I am beyond what you think of me or even what I have, in the past, thought of me.

In our complete yielding to God, we become. There it is, so simple really. We become. It is not about the outer world's opinion any more, yet it is the outer world we are here to serve in our becoming. We are supported by the Kingdom of God, and finally, we are truly free.

Affirmation:

I behold the Divine Light within me. I'm grateful and thankful for who I've become.

I Trust in Thee

The Lord is my shepherd; I shall not want. He maketh me to lie down in green pastures; he leadeth me beside the still waters...

Holy Bible, Psalm 23

Over the years, my little mind has been working overtime to make sure that I and my body of affairs would be all right, but lately I seem to have found a better way. I suddenly feel relieved of a burden that's been too large to carry anyway. I must have said a million times that I'm going to turn it over to God, but then didn't do it. I thought I had, but clearly I was still working hard controlling everything to keep myself safe.

Lately, though, I notice that I'm feeling happy and thankful most of the time. I seem to have let go of all the things I've been worrying about and instead just seem to be focusing on the vision—the beautiful dream of my life.

Everything is going to be all right, yet nothing has changed in my external world. I've just given up the internal struggle to think I could change things by my worrying, that somehow I could handle my big life all by myself. Now I trust God; God will handle it. Because my thoughts are creative, now I'm assisting and accelerating the process of my own dramatic unfoldment rather than getting in the way of it.

Thank you, Divine Spirit, whatever and wherever you are. Thank you for relieving me of my burden. I'm free now to slow down and love more. There is an inner knowing that all is well. The right words will come; my needs—all of them—will be met.

I've reached a new level of surrender, and I'm embodying a deeper trust and faith. "The Lord is my shepherd; I shall not want." In gratitude and thanksgiving, I remain.

Affirmation:

I am fueled by the love of God! I rejoice in my life and see only beauty before me!

Authenticity

When you have obtained the smallest demonstration...you have experienced something that never leaves you. You have the witness of Truth within yourself, and this is the only authority worth having.

Emmet Fox

What a valued commodity! Sometimes as we move up the ladder of successful living it becomes more and more important that we be liked and admired. Our ego finds it advantageous to say and do what pleases others—at the sacrifice of our own authenticity. We become people pleasers and, let's face it, it does seem to have its rewards. If I agree with you and do what you like, I've convinced myself that you will love me and accept me. Then I'm home free or so I think. I don't even notice that I've lost myself so completely to the outside world that I don't even know who I am any more.

But then we hit upon the great question "Who am I?" and we are thrown for a loop. We realize that we have sacrificed what we believed in and have denied ourselves our own loving. We have lost contact with our true essence. We've lost contact with that part of us which makes us so unique and special; we've lost contact with who we are as a spiritual being.

Truth is a beautiful thing, and it's a delight when you learn to deliver it lovingly. I've come to see that people appreciate the truth. It is so refreshing in a world filled with people pleasers, subterfuge and manipulation. What is true for you is important for your own peace of mind and harmony. What is true for you is the doorway to your own self-love and Being.

We are here to know our Loving Essence, to declare ourselves Authentic Being and Light of the World. We don't have to be someone else to be loved. We are made in the image and likeness of God and that is quite enough!

Affirmation:

I declare myself Loving Essence! I am Authentic Being and Light of the World!

The Blessing of Holidays

For what the heart feels and believes, the words are sure to speak forth.

Emma Curtis Hopkins

I love that I love. I love that there is so much to love. There is a time of year when everyone is softer—the feeling of gratitude is in the air. It lasts recognizably from Thanksgiving time through Christmas. We can't help ourselves—the feeling is in the air, and we get to bask in it.

Even those of us with very little resources can find the joy and gratitude even when we can't see it during the rest of the year. There is the gentleness of acceptance and allowing. Our attention is brought there by the media and everything around us—it makes us focus on a kinder, gentler way. We feel softer, happier, more loving, and all that has really happened is a change of mind. Our consciousness has shifted and it shows up in form here and there and everywhere—the holidays—a time to celebrate and rejoice.

Wouldn't it be wonderful if we could focus our attention on gratitude, love and peace all the time, not just in November and December? It's a choice you know. Nothing is stopping us. Whatever we find to be grateful for during the holiday time is just as true year round. We're just not paying attention to it.

There is so much goodness and beauty everywhere. It's not hard to find. Look for it and you will see it. The more you love, the more you are loved. The more you are thankful, the more you have to be thankful for. The more you have peace in your heart, the more peace will appear all around you. It's up to you. Thankfully, it's all a sweet decision.

Affirmation:

With love in my heart and eyes to see, everything is working together for my good.

What's New?

As human beings, our greatness lies not so much in being able to remake the world... as in being able to remake ourselves.

Mahatma Gandhi

How about you? What if you made a decision that this year would be like no other? What if you made a decision that you would be more loving this year than ever before? What if you decided—oh can it be—that you are worth loving?

I think so many of us doubt our lovability. It seems to be a human condition... am I good enough? Do I deserve to be loved? I am here to tell you, the answer is yes! You are worthy of great love. You are quite lovable.

If we could just capture the preciousness of our lives—the way God sees us and has always seen us, we would doubt ourselves never again. We would love ourselves for all eternity! That is where it all begins, for when we can truly understand that we are beloved because we are the Beloved of God, then we can start living the life we intended to live when we chose this human incarnation.

We would stop playing small because we are not small. We are here to be big for God. Once we understand who we truly are, we see it everywhere and in everyone.

We become a beneficial presence on the planet. We really begin to make a difference because we are not desperately trying to get something. We become great givers and great servants. We are in the Divine flow; we see that the more we give, the more we receive.

Life is a blessing! We are a blessing! Become a New You. Don't waste a moment more of your great life!

Affirmation:

I am made brand new! The love in my heart expands and I live in the ever-expanding good of God!

To Love

Do not spill thy soul; do not all descend; keep thy state; stay at home in thine own heaven.

Emerson

Sometimes it feels that we've lost our way. We somehow have drifted into thought forms of separation. As is the way of Love Intelligence for those of us who have made spiritual practice our life, suddenly we reunite with the Source of all good, and we remember why we are here.

Ah, to love—to feel the love and to be the love. How could I have forgotten how tender God's love is within me? How could I forget that I'm never alone. The Great God Almighty loves me and cherishes me as It does all of us. I live in the vastness of Its love. Rickie Byars-Beckwith's song reminds us, "Return to me, return to me. With every breath, return." I remember now, I'm God's Beloved. There is a Divine conspiracy on my behalf. As I recognize myself, I see myself in all others. Love-beauty everywhere—the great testament to God's pure love. In the quiet, I remember my Source and my heart overflows.

Through God all things will come. In the moment of doubt, in the moment of sadness, in the moment of pain, return to me. In me is your comfort. It is good to be steeped in Spirit, to have a level of spiritual practice so that I don't get snagged or caught up in my forgetfulness. So many thoughts come and go, yet I keep my eye single upon God, seeking first the Kingdom of Heaven, knowing that all else will be added.

My devotion becomes a steadying, life-giving force in my life. I have chosen well and I can rest in peace.

Affirmation:

I joyously expand my capacity for love. I am set free in my willingness to love more.

Ignorance is Bliss

Beginner's mind is Zen practice in action. It is the mind that is innocent of preconceptions and expectations, judgments and prejudices. Beginner's mind is just present to explore and observe and see "things as-they-are."

Abbess Zenkei Blanche Hartman

Sometimes we know too much for our own good. The greatest blessing for me in this, my first ministry, is that I don't know anything about it. It's like your first love. There is something special about your first love. You are innocent, and the mind is not filled with all the reasons why things might not work out. All I know is how much I love this Universal Intelligence I call God and how much it loves me. My best recourse then is to turn in Its direction. Through meditation and prayer, surrender, faith and trust, all is revealed, and the miracles come.

This is it. We come to the awareness that we know nothing compared to the Infinite Mind of God. We know nothing. The mind is emptied. We are in the beginner's mind, like the first love rather than the mind we bring to our fourth or fifth marriage. With the surrender, faith and trust of the beginner's mind, we are in the flow. It is so much more effective and powerful operating from spiritual wisdom rather than our human intellect. My friend said to me that she can see that her small son is perfect in every way. It's only when she or someone else dumps their stuff on him that he has a problem. Otherwise, he is innocent. I'm sure that's why Jesus suggested, "Be ye as little children."

So we have to work a little bit at emptying the mind. It has been so filled with all that misinformation about our worthiness and how the world works. We can trust our inner wisdom as we were birthed a Divine emanation of the one and only God. We are guided and directed always as the Beloved in whom God is so well pleased.

Affirmation:

I yield to God and let go of my need to know! I joyously open my mind and heart to infinite wisdom!

Keep Dancing

The true self includes the inner and higher self which is always in immediate touch with the Great Divine Mind.

Thomas Troward

In truth, I think we are destined to be opened by the living of our days. We live our joys and we live our sorrows and hopefully through it all, we come into the full awareness of who we are as authentic being.

Sometimes we are called further into experience than we'd like to go, but it is such times that allow us to discover what it means to be truly alive. Our darkest moments can bring us into our most brilliant authenticity. This is the nature of life.

Through the good times and the bad, we are sustained by an indomitable Spirit within us—the fire of our inner essence. No matter what we are facing, there is something within us that is resilient and solid. In our joys and in our sorrows, we live from this inner strength and fortitude. No matter what shows up in our lives, we can know that there is a part of us that will never be defeated. There is a grace that comes forth in us whenever we are challenged.

It is this Spirit within that makes life worth living...that allows us to realize the blessing of life itself. It assures us that if we just keep on dancing, we'll be all right—that the possibility of glory days are just ahead. We can be fearless, no matter what, and know completely and forever that we are tuned in and tapped into a great and mighty power that wants only our joy and happiness.

What we realize is that there is more to this business of living than we can possibly know—maybe even in one lifetime. Once the crisis that opens us passes, will we continue such authentic living? It seems our only job is to keep on dancing.

Affirmation:

My power lives within me. Things come, things go, but the power of God in me loves, sustains and supports me always!

The Best is Yet to Come

Rest calm and serene—you are safe and protected by the Infinite Power of the Father-Mother Mind. Within the Father-Mother Mind, mortal children are at home.

The Kybalion

In continuously opening to the infinite possibility for our lives, how can it be otherwise? New desire is generated in us all the time. It is that desire that sends us into the new territory. We trust Spirit, and it brings us onto the higher ground.

We were born for greatness… oh, I'm not talking about some role we play for public adulation. I'm talking about the Living Spirit within each and every one of us, the Spirit that is of Divine Mind. We were not born to play small, to judge and criticize our neighbor, to be bored out of our minds. We came to love and serve a greater idea. Some of us have gotten quite caught up in the minutia of daily living. We have forgotten that we have a choice about the quality of our days, that we can make a decision the minute our eyes open in the early morning hours. This is going to be the best day of my life! We have forgotten about the creative power that lies within us, that we are not a victim of anything.

I'm not saying that living a great life does not require courage sometimes… and faith and trust. When the world around us seems to be going amuck, our job is to stay the course, hold the high watch, keep our vision strong, pray and meditate, keeping our eye single upon all that is good and holy. We keep our eye single upon the new world—a world filled with peace, joy and love and we become that.

The best is yet to come. That is an excellent vision to hold for ourselves and for our world. The best is yet to come. Do not fear for anything for the Great God of Love is everywhere!

Affirmation:

I stand firm in my love of God, my love of life, and the miracle of infinite possibility!

My Papa

The highest state of evolution has always been in the person who has directly sensed God in self and self in God.

Ernest Holmes

In my life, I did not know a loving and safe human father. That was a great loss for me. They say we choose. I don't know why I would choose something that would cause me so much pain.

But today, ah today, I have many fathers. I can pick and choose from the very best, and there are so many of them. And there is the great Father in all of us, just as there is the great Mother. We are connected one to another in an abundance of goodness.

My great Papa, as near as my hands and feet, loves me completely, would never forsake me or judge me. He is, as I am, the strength within me. What a gift to know that I can be renewed by the renewing of my own mind—that today, I can choose to surround myself with loving father energy, both human and divine.

That burning flame within us cannot be extinguished, no matter what the outer conditions of our life. The flame burns bright, reminding us that we are not a victim of anything. When we have cleared the cobwebs away enough to hear the good news of God, we are assured of our pure radiance as Divine Being.

We see that forever and always, we are loved. We are cherished beyond belief. We are worshipped in our holiness. We come into this human life full of beauty and full of light, and that's all we really have to remember. We were born, and will always remain, Divine Perfect Love.

Affirmation:

I am the radiance of Pure Spirit! My life is a holy one! There is goodness all around me!

It's No Thing

In one atom are found all the elements of the earth; in one motion of the mind are found all the motions of existence; in one drop of water are found all the secrets of the endless oceans; in one aspect of you are found all the aspects of life.

Kahlil Gibran

Sometimes we think we have separate issues going on simultaneously whether it's a situation at work, something going on in your relationship at home, the diminishment of your finances or a threat to your health… you name it. I have finally embodied a simple truth. There are no separate issues to deal with out there in life. It is all one issue: How deeply can I love? Am I willing to take a deep, personal, penetrating inner look at my life and who I am and do some healing work—most of it coming down to one thing—am I worthy and willing to become love completely?

I'm not talking about the limited and conditional kind of love we experience at the personality level. I'm talking about the kind of love that allows one to say "I am the way, the truth and the life."

When you become love like that, you realize that all issues in the outer world are the same issue and are solved by, dare I say it, BECOMING LOVE. When issues arise (and they do) and I am upset by something, I sit still until the presence of love is all I feel inside of me and all is resolved. My way is made clear, and I am then able to speak and take all action from a loving place.

Life becomes easier and filled with grace, love and joy. Everything can be resolved, and all at once, by the love that is anchored so deeply within.

I am the way, the truth and the life. I AM.

Affirmation:

All my concerns are dissolved in my willingness to know only love as my life!

A Seed Upon the Wind with God

Man without God is a seed upon the wind… It means that such a man has no sense of center. He is at home nowhere because he is not at home somewhere.

Howard Thurman, *For the Inward Journey*

When I read this writing from Howard Thurman, I realized that this is the journey most of us take as we consciously evolve. Most of us begin as a seed upon the wind without God and if we continue our spiritual practice long enough and earnestly enough, we become a seed upon the wind with God.

Very soon after our arrival in human form, we forget who we are, thanks to the intense domestication (Don Miguel Ruiz's word) we experience from our parents, teachers and others in our outer world. We are then at the effect of the outer world. If things are good there, we are good. If not, we suffer. We are at the mercy of forces beyond our control.

If we stay with our spiritual work and practice long enough, however, soon enough there comes a complete surrender, a commitment and a yielding to God at the core of our being and our life takes on new meaning. We become an open vessel for God's expression. We become God's own. We are not afraid then; the fear of living is gone.

We are now motivated by faith, not fear. We are in a continual state of love because we become it. Our lack of attachment to outcome makes us as a seed—we may be here or we may be there, as the God Presence moves through and as us. Life is good because God is good. Our life takes on a greater purpose than our small ends.

This is the nature of our conscious evolution. It does not come without struggle, but being a seed upon the wind with God allows us to experience love, joy and absolute freedom unlike anything we have ever known.

Affirmation:

I am a seed upon the wind with God. I am love. I am joy. I am free.

Sweet Peace

I will love thee, O Lord, my strength and my trust.

Holy Bible, Psalm 18:1

The heart is full. God is my rock, my fortress and my deliverer, my strength and my shield. God is the horn of my salvation and my high tower. Everywhere I am, there It is.

When I contemplate the love of God, all is right in my world. All is peaceful. All is sacred. All is holy. In the freshness of the morning hours, my mind is quiet. Breathing in and breathing out, more and more peace lives in the midst of me. I rest in the stillness, so grateful for this blessed encounter with my authentic Self.

This is the truth of my being. There is nothing to push against. In this moment, I am an opening for greater expression. The tightness of trying to protect myself from whatever I might fear is dissolved. I am free to be me; but it is an awakened, vibrant me! I am fearless and yet a participant in the world along with everyone else. I have nothing to prove to anyone.

Oh Sweet Spirit, can I possibly contain more? That would be my only desire—to be more of Love. This is bliss—to know myself as

Love so completely, to be so fearless, and to know that all is right in my world. Everything is taken care of. I am my true self.

So much to be grateful for, so much to praise God for, so good to be so true. Peace Beloveds, Sweet Peace.

Affirmation:

I awake to my true identity as Divine Spirit. I will love thee, O God, my strength and my trust.

The Divine Miracle

Every person, all the events of your life are there because you have drawn them there. What you choose to do with them is up to you.

Richard Bach

Oh my Beloveds, there is nothing that happens in your life that is not an opportunity for great learning. There is life happening and then there is the spiritual truth in each and every situation. In that perfection is the process of our inner evolution. When you can begin to see your life from that spiritual perspective, you will be set free! You will experience heaven on earth. In that, you will find your joy and your salvation. That is how amazing and good God is. We are given opportunity after opportunity to reveal the truth of our being.

It is for you to understand that nothing happens as a punishment but rather as a lesson. It is our birthright that we should learn and grow from life. It doesn't matter what the circumstance, look for the spiritual truth. Look for the light behind every bit of darkness. We are here to learn and grow and to become. There are no accidents. When we realize that everything is happening for our spiritual growth, we can ask "What am I to learn from this?" "What possible good is in this situation?"

To remember our true identity as Divine Spirit—this is the human walk—the human experience... to find God in all things. How grateful I am to be on this sacred journey of self discovery with you. Let us be excited together at the prospect of tomorrow. Let us thank God and joyfully welcome our own becoming.

Affirmation:

Today I move to a new place in consciousness. I release old limiting ideas and turn to new ways of being. I allow the great revelation to begin.

The Seven-Day Mental Diet

And be not conformed to this world, but be ye transformed by the renewing of your mind...

Holy Bible, Romans 12:2

I'm in the process of mastering my mind. It began when I put myself and my congregation on a seven-day mental diet. We were to refrain from dwelling on negative thoughts for seven days. In our human experience, thoughts come in often and some (or all, depending on where you're standing) are negative. The key is to be able to catch when you are giving negative thoughts a roosting place. An analogy is when a hot cinder falls on your shirt sleeve. If you flick it off immediately, it doesn't have time to do any damage. If you leave it there, the damage is done.

For me, this became mind mastery at its finest. When I found myself obsessing on something negative, I would think instead of something for which I was grateful. I discovered that I am able to hang out in bliss most of the time and, as a result, more good stuff is coming into my life. Seven days is long enough to begin to develop a habit of positive thinking.

Oh yes, living a great life requires discipline... discipline to do the things that you know are going to create the life you want to live.

We are in bondage to nothing except our own faulty thinking. Once we take charge of our life and begin to do the things that we know are for our highest good, everything and everyone transforms right before our eyes.

I invite you to try the seven-day mental diet. You will find out things about yourself in the process. Some of you will discover that you like singing the blues or that feeling good is not worth the effort. On the other hand, some of you might find a life of bliss. How good is that!

Affirmation:

I behold the goodness all around me. I am looking through the eyes of Love.

Behold the Christ Presence in You

Love is a fire; I am wood.

Rumi

We may think we suffer because of lack of love from others, but that is NEVER THE CASE. Our suffering actually comes from not loving ourselves. Nothing is more painful than that.

I read somewhere that self-love is like food for the starving. As you begin to feel your own love, you realize how much energy you've put into trying to get love on the outside and how, no matter how much of that you've received from someone else, it's never been enough. That's because it doesn't change your inner beliefs. If another person says you're wonderful and on a core level you don't believe it, their love will only be a temporary fix. Soon enough, you will be looking for more from them or someone else. Only self-love will fill up the emptiness inside of you that stems from your false belief that you are unlovable.

Everything in your life is going to reflect back to you this lack of love for yourself. If you are wounded inside and haven't addressed those wounded places, they will out-picture in those around you. Life is like a mirror.

Self-love is vital to our well-being. If I say I am Spirit in the flesh, how can I not love God as me? How can I not have compassion for my God-self? When we realize who we are as Divine Being, loving the Self is not a selfish act. It is action which assures our walk in the world as a beneficial presence.

Look into the mirror and behold the Christ Presence in you. In humility, be grateful that so much love has been planted within you. You are not to waste it. You are to love and be loved.

Affirmation:

My loving is assured! I spread my wings and fly!

The Perfection in the Imperfection

As human beings, our greatness lies not so much in being able to remake the world—that is the myth of the atomic age—as in being able to remake ourselves.

Mahatma Gandhi

One morning at 3:30 a.m. I awoke with a sudden awareness of how perfect I've tried to be all my life. I think it comes from being raised in a pretty dysfunctional family and trying to pretend that it wasn't happening. What was my message? Keep a good face on it, try to be as good as you can, and no one will know the truth.

All my protective devices are shattering now in the face of the love I'm becoming. The last holdout is my ability to love myself deeply. Can I love myself enough, knowing all my imperfections? I think back now at how hard I've been on myself and of course on those around me.

Here's the truth. You—me—all of us are perfect at core. We've always been perfect. We were born as perfection itself. In the beginning and when all is said and done, we are lovable and worthy of love just because we exist. We don't have to prove that to anyone. Through our faulty thinking, though, many of us have spent a lifetime living in opposition to our true nature. Most people say, when asked their deepest truth, that they don't feel good enough—that they are not worthy.

As God's Beloved, you are no less brilliant than the stars in the sky, no less deserving. When we really begin to remember who we are as love itself—mistakes, imperfections and all—we will understand how to love another. I'm holding nothing back in my own becoming. I embrace myself as the Beloved of God, perfect in my imperfection, and now I'm free to see the perfection in you!

Affirmation:

I release all judgment against myself and all others. I see the face of God everywhere.

The New Christology

When the Fall is dismissed, traditional Christology cannot help but go with it and a new Christology must emerge, as a phoenix rising from the ashes of the past.

Bishop John Shelby Spong, *Sins of Scripture*

Bishop Spong further states, "It will be a Christology based not on fall and rescue, sin and salvation or even guilt and forgiveness, but on the call to wholeness, the power of love and the enhancement of being." These words of Bishop Spong are powerful!

There is a new paradigm for new times. Nothing is the same. We can no longer live in the past with our old ideas and precepts about the world and the nature of God.

We, as New Thought Ancient Wisdom practitioners of truth, are poised in just the right place. Willing to open ourselves completely in trust and faith and a yielding into our Divine Self, the loving God of our knowing can express through and as us, and the world meets a new God and a new truth. It meets the new Christology.

This is a significant time in our history. We are facing challenges, but they are necessary for the evolution of our individual and collective consciousness. The challenges of the times force us to awaken spiritually, but back of all of it is our loving God, the Love Intelligence that created all things and that which is seeking to emerge mightily within us.

Standing in a place of strong inner knowing and conviction, we can ride the tide of the shifting times unafraid and excited at the prospect of a new world order. Through our own Becoming, we participate as a beneficial presence in the reshaping and redefining that is taking place in this world of effects. Our participation as love itself is an imperative. We go back to the beginning, our own Becoming, when Being was as important as Doing.

Simply, we return to God!

Affirmation:

My faith is strengthened and I open myself completely to my own Divine awakening!

I Am What Thou Art

Oh, that thou wouldest bless me indeed, and enlarge my coast, and that thine hand might be with me, and that thou wouldest keep me from evil, that it may not grieve me!

Holy Bible, 1 Chronicles 4:10

Whether we know it consciously or not, when we gain anything at the expense of another, we have dishonored the self. It happens when we get caught in the mesmerism of the human condition, allowing our ego to take over. We forget who we are as divine beings. We forget that we cannot harm another without harming the self; for at the core of our being, we are only one living presence. That is why revenge never works, because we hurt ourselves in the process, even though it may seem otherwise. You cannot fool the Indwelling Presence whose very nature is utmost integrity! You, awakened in this physical expression, are called to the highest form of integrity. When you recognize your true identity, being out of integrity is uncomfortable at the least, and very painful at its worst.

The desire of the heart, as we attempt to lead a God-ordained life, is to be clear and free inside from anything unlike God. We are tuned in and alert to the times when we are out of alignment with the Essential Self. The invitation at that moment is to take the necessary action to free ourselves once again to be a place of unconditional love. We hear and can follow the guidance that is given from within. Then, joyfully, life becomes a sacred everyday experience! We are tuned in and turned on. We are blessed as open channels for Holy Communion with Spirit.

In this freedom, I am what Thou art. I am willing to live in utmost integrity. I can trust and be trusted and I am set free from judgment of myself or others. Love and peace are my life. I do not fight against myself.

Affirmation:

My source is within me! All my needs are met in time and on time! I need not fear anything for I am unconditional love expressing everywhere!

The Answer

(Wo)man is a spark from a great fire which is God.

Emmet Fox

Because we live in the human experience, no matter how much inner work we've done, there will be times when troubles loom, that we get caught in the world of appearances. We will know it pretty quickly because of the unfamiliar feeling of our own suffering.

There is only one answer to the difficult problems in life and that is turning within to God. In other words, in times of need, our greatest comfort and the answer to our dilemma will come from our ability to realign ourselves with the Creator of All Good, God. We realign ourselves without knowing the resolution to our dilemma. This action takes great trust and faith, but each time we do it, and our prayer is answered in some miraculous way, our faith and trust are deepened. We have confirmation that we are right on track, that indeed God will see us through no matter the difficulty.

As a result, our love and devotion to God grows mightily. It is confirmed—yes, this is a loving universe. Yes, I am the Beloved. Yes, if I trust in God and have faith, my prayers will be answered and my needs will be met. I feel and sense beyond a shadow of a doubt how much I am loved. I can see the light and feel God at work in and through me.

As I practice living in faith and trust, the times between my lapse into fear and my return to conscious living grow shorter. I'm grateful for my own awareness because there is so much less pain and suffering in the awakened state. In appreciation and gratitude for that knowing, I willingly surrender even more into my own grace and glory, and I am set free.

Affirmation:

Peace is my name and nature. I am love in action.

Love's Great Example

Very few people understand the heart. In truth, your heart is one of the masterpieces of creation.

Michael A. Singer, *The Untethered Soul*

There is a great call now for us to discover our own holiness. Jesus was our great example. That is why we speak of him 2000 plus years later. When we understand the Divine Light within us and align with it as he did, we touch and experience that holiness. We can understand why he would say "Thou shalt love thy neighbor as thyself." (Mark 12:31)

Most of us have experienced it at one time or another—an opening of the heart—a complete yielding into something greater that created a feeling within us of absolute incredible beauty. We might have felt it while witnessing something breathtaking in nature, or at the birth of a baby or in the ecstasy of making love. That is the experience of living in Oneness.

A greater and greater expression of that feeling of oneness is being birthed on the planet right now. Its power is exponential. It can allay all our fears. It can lead us and show us the way to individual and universal peace and harmony. When we experience our own holiness, we are suddenly able to listen and hear what is being said and there is a desire within to reach an understanding. We find our similarities and gravitate to what is the same about us.

The great transformation that is happening in this world right now begins within our own soul. There is nothing to fix outside of us. We are here to discover our own nature as Love Itself. This can be the year we come home to Self. It will be the best year of our lives when we finally discover that what we've been seeking outside of ourselves has been here all along.

This is the perfect year to bless you and say, "Welcome Home!"

Affirmation:

I embrace the Love I am. I come home to my own holiness.

Keep Thine Eye Single

The light of the body is the eye: if therefore thine eye be single, thy whole body shall be full of light.

Holy Bible, Matthew 6:22

No matter what is going on in the world around us, no matter what challenges we face... and our human experience dictates that we will face some in the course of our life... we must remember to keep our eye focused on the goodness of God. In that is our comfort. In that is our salvation. When we are reminded of that truth and sit in the stillness in contemplation of that, we can find peace in the midst of chaos. We can find answers to problems that seemed impossible to solve. We don't have to know the "how." We just have to trust and have faith that God's goodness will see us through.

This is true even in the darkest, most frightening times and in situations when we feel most alone. There is a great Presence and Power available to us. It is not missing; we have simply fallen asleep to it. We sometimes think it's hard to find God, when in reality, it is impossible to avoid God. God as Spirit is everywhere, equally present and accessible at all times. It is we who sometimes forget. When we finally remember to lean into our spiritual practice, to sit quietly in the stillness, we find that we are strengthened inwardly. We remember that we are never alone, that there is a powerful force for good in the midst of us. Our life is a holy one and in grace, the light appears. We are reminded of our connection to all that is good and true, and we are empowered and set free from feelings of helplessness.

How good God is! It is our salvation. It is our light. Now I can see God everywhere and I remember the oneness of all life!

Affirmation:

My life is a holy one! I remember that I am supported in a loving universe!

Your Self Realized

When you realize there is nothing lacking, the whole world belongs to you.

Lao Tzu

The thing that we look with is the thing we have been looking for.

Ernest Holmes, *The Science of Mind*

What a difference in your life when you wake up to who you are as Love Itself. You begin to see that so much of your giving was about getting. You realize that for most of your life, you have been in the care and feeding of your ego. There's a part of you that is ego driven; there's a part of you that knows all about that...what you are doing and why; and then there's a part of you that you discover if you are persevering enough that is filled full with love and complete in every way.

Here I am in my gratitude, understanding that my greatest and perhaps only purpose for being in this physical body is to love. My eyes see love where I couldn't see it before. Everything softens in my gaze. I rest more in my being, opening up in my desire for inclusion. I now see that no one is outside the circle of God's unconditional love. My love is reflected back to me in all forms. I am assisted in unexpected ways. I'm living in the mystery, yet feeling absolutely guided and protected—finally safe, not realizing how long I've been striving to feel safe.

The blessings are everywhere—the beauty, the love, the joy! I am filled to overflowing with the prosperity and abundance of this world. In that, I am set free.

Affirmation:

I choose to see God in myself and in every person I meet. I choose to bring God out into the open for all to see and celebrate!

Reconciliation

A sense of separation from God is the only lack you really need correct.

A Course in Miracles

There is an angel on my shoulder. I was meeting with two strong-willed individuals, and I wanted them to be able to work together and appreciate one another. The Dalai Lama says the greatest challenge facing the world now is to realize our oneness. It doesn't matter whether we are two major factions in conflict in the Middle East or two strong-willed individuals destined to work together in the little town of Ojai, California. What can we focus upon that will open the hearts? It will surely not be our differences. It will be the place inside of us that can recognize each other and realize our sameness. No matter how far apart our egos have taken us, in the end, there is that within us which never separates itself from the other. How do we come together in that place?

That's where the power is. That's where all things are possible. The walls of defense come down; the heart opens. There is nothing to push against. We no longer feel threatened and we don't have to protect ourselves. Now we can build upon what we know about each other that reminds us of ourselves. I see you, but most importantly, I see myself in you. I can now see your strengths and your heart.

I'm not afraid of you any more—that you will try to hurt me or take something from me. I see that there is more than enough. A surprise is that great personal healing can take place in the name of another. The hearts expand in harmony and remembrance.

That's the answer for reconciliation on all levels. How can I become quiet enough to listen to my own heart? When I do that, I am guided and directed in the most perfect ways. Thank you God for loving us so much!

Affirmation:

I surrender completely to the power and presence of God within me!

Celebrating the Christ Presence

Everything which you can conceive and accept is yours! Entertain no doubt. Refuse to accept worry or hurry or fear. That which knows and does everything is inside you and harkens to the slightest whisper.

Uell Stanley Andersen

The great one who was Jesus knew that the creative Source of the universe is in the words "I am that I am." He knew God as the Source of all good and further that the Spirit of God is within each and every one of us. Jesus said, "Verily, verily, I say unto you, he that believeth on me, the works that I do shall he do also; and greater works than these shall he do…" (John 14:12)

I've come into a new and deeper awareness of just how powerful I am—how powerful we all are as Divine Creative Beings of Light. Most of us do not use that power, however; we give it away, not knowing that in the realization of that power, miracles become an every day occurrence. Rather than praying to a God outside myself who is gong to answer my prayers, I realize that the power for answered prayer lies within me. I am the prayer and I am the answer.

How can we claim that much power? Perhaps it is easier for us when we realize that God is Love. We are Love. Further, this Source I know is delighted by the deepening of the awareness of the Spirit within. I and my Father/Mother God are one—it is a holy sacred union as is all of life.

Do not think it blasphemy to love God that much—to become Love Itself—to become that powerful. We are to rejoice in the celebration of the Christ Presence within! I am that I am!

Affirmation:

Thank you Divine Source that I may love myself enough to see the sacred and holy in me!

Love, the Great Equalizer

That they all may be one; as thou, Father, art in me, and I in thee, that they also may be one in us... I in them, and thou in me, that they may be made perfect in one...

Holy Bible, John 17:21-23

To see the soul of another is an amazing gift. To look into someone's eyes and see the perfection there is a sacred experience. That is transcendent love. It's not the conditional love we are so used to experiencing in this human realm. It is the realization that I am you and you are me. Something great has transpired between us—a liberation of consciousness that allows me to see how completely interconnected we all are. That I can experience this in myself is the beginning of the healing of the world.

Once I can truly see you and understand you from the place of our similarities, my compassion grows. I can forgive you and ask for your forgiveness. Until all this happens, we are living on the very surface of life. We are not diving in deep. We are skirting the edge of infinite possibility.

Conditional relationships are not easy. They require lots of intense navigation and manipulation. "I will be happy if you just change and do what I say." My happiness becomes dependent upon your cooperation with me. What would it feel like for me to be responsible for my own happiness? Once I recognize and begin to truly love my Self (not from the ego's perspective), I am set free and I can set you free.

We are here to discover the beautiful radiant love and light that is within all of us. It is the Christ Presence—Love Itself. It is the road to true freedom and liberation. It is there awaiting your recognition of it. As a gift to yourself, I welcome you to come home to the Self.

Affirmation:

I celebrate the Christ Presence within me. It is the radiant wholeness and perfection that is my life. I walk in love and joy!

The Greatest Story Ever Told

In my defenselessness, my safety lies.

Course in Miracles, Lesson 153

The crucifixion and resurrection story has become the greatest story ever told because while on the cross, Jesus made a decision to keep his heart open. "Father, forgive them, for they know not what they do." If he had yelled out some hate-filled words, there would have been no story. As a practitioner of truth that is our charge—to choose love no matter the circumstance, and that is a high order. It is so much easier to give as good as you get—to respond to attack with attack.

As we practice choosing love, we discover that there is a place we come to inside of us which is defenseless. What allowed Jesus to be triumphant was his willingness to be in the love no matter what was happening to him. He knew that defenselessness was strength. It was the recognition of the Christ Presence within him; and in that, he knew his power.

The Christ Presence within us can see us through any adversity. When we experience that great transcendent love that is in the midst of us, we truly become defenseless, and in that is our greatest power.

282

We begin to see that there is nothing to defend against. I am you and you are me. I see the perfection in you, even when you can't see it for yourself.

It takes great courage and personal strength to remain centered when all seems to be going wrong around us and we feel under attack. Just know that when we are in the midst of loss, betrayal or crisis of any kind, we can do as Jesus did, turn to the Christ Presence within and know that Magnificent Love will see us through. Be still and know that I am God in the midst of you.

Affirmation:

I am sheltered and safe in the loving arms of God. I turn within to the Christ Presence and know that all is well.

Your Faith Will Make You Whole

We must trust the Invisible, for it is the soul cause of that which is visible.

Ernest Holmes, *The Science of Mind*

Here I sit at the Casa de Dom Inacio in Abadiania, Brazil, having just spent several days in the presence of John of God. People come here from all over the world to be healed of whatever may be ailing them. John credits himself only with being a medium through which various spirits do their work. He is surrounded in the room by 25 huge crystals, some of which are four feet tall and several feet wide as well. The room where he sits to do the work is filled with believers from all walks of life, people who don't speak the same language as I do, and I find myself surrounded by people who have come here with great faith in something that they cannot see. Sitting here has made me appreciate the power of faith. I have discovered that faith of this kind can move mountains. Through our faith, we are made whole. Through our faith, love shows up and healings of all kinds happen. Through our faith, we find peace on earth and immeasurable joy.

It's not so easy for some to have faith in what they cannot see, and unfortunately or fortunately, however you choose to perceive it, faith provides its own proof. If you sit on the outside of real life as a doubting Thomas, you will never receive the evidence you've needed to allow yourself to step into the circle of God's unconditional love.

But as I sit here, experiencing the love of my being, I find Heaven on Earth. All pales in comparison. You can begin even with faith as small as a mustard seed. Begin there and you will find your way to perfect love and perfect peace!

Affirmation:

I am love, and I rest now in the silence, realizing that the love I am is the love I give and the love I receive. All there is, is Love!

Unstoppable!

I skate to where the puck will be, not to where it has been.

Wayne Gretzky

In his simple statement, Wayne is giving us a formula for inspired, wholehearted living. So many of us place our attention on what has happened in the past and we get stuck in our own limited thinking about the possibilities for the future. This is all I've ever done so this is what I'm capable of and no more. The fact is, however, when you keep your eye focused on the infinite possibility of each now moment, anything is possible. As we like to say, principle is not bound by precedent.

It doesn't matter what has happened up to this moment—that is history. It's over. What matters is what you are holding in your consciousness as to the possibility for your life now. That's how we stretch and grow into the next evolution. Keep thy eye single upon the infinite nature of this universe and there is no telling what might happen next. As we begin to live from that kind of openness and allowing, we move into the flow—you can imagine the flow of Wayne Gretzky as he rockets across the ice—he is unstoppable!

What I'm abundantly clear about is that everything we desire is already here. If we are not seeing it, we are in our own way. We are the ones blocking our good. The universe does not do that. We are here to keep our eye single upon the prize—to feel it and experience it with all our senses. Wayne keeps his eye single upon the puck going into the goal and he is always one step ahead of the game.

We, too, want to be one step ahead of the game. Just as Wayne does, we can see ourselves rocketing toward our own personal great prize and we declare ourselves unstoppable champions of this game of life!

Affirmation:

I am fully engaged in wholehearted living! I am unstoppable as I rocket into greater fulfillment! I am that I am!

The Forgiving Heart

If we wish to change what we are experiencing, we must change what we are.

Orrin Moen

My mission in life is to free myself from any thoughts or belief systems that would limit me or block me from being an open channel for good.

Unfortunately, sometimes there are things buried so deep inside us in our subconscious mind, we don't know of their existence but they are running our life nonetheless.

In ancient times, the Hawaiians spoke a prayer of reconciliation and forgiveness whose intention was just that—to heal us and to remove any obstacles to being a pure channel for God's love and supply. The practice is called Ho'oponopono and it can empty us out and bring us back to the purity of our Divine Self. I speak this prayer now as a daily practice. "I'm sorry. Please forgive me. I love you. Thank you." I speak it when a part of my body needs healing, when I see something in someone else which annoys me and would cause me to judge or be harmful in my mind or when I am judging myself or am negative and out of sorts.

This prayer covers the bases. It's a cleansing of our interior landscape and will set us free if we let it. Not only does it set us free. It sets others in our experience free also.

I send this prayer of love out to you. "I'm sorry. Please forgive me. I love you. Thank you."

Affirmation:

My life is holy and I free myself completely from all that is unholy.

Now I Can See the Moon

Barn's burnt down… now I can see the moon.

Masahide

Our busy lives are so full of distractions, sometimes the worst has to happen for us to get a glimpse of what is "Real." We can be brought to our knees, but like the moon, Spirit is always there, never deserting us. Sometimes it's necessary for something as catastrophic as the barn burning for us to find our way back home. Something becomes visible to us that we could not have seen before.

This is the story of life. We will probably face many "barn burnings" but how comforting to know that like the moon, Spirit is always there, awaiting our recognition of it. Spirit will never desert us no matter how great the devastation. We can turn in Its direction and find comfort. It may be terrifying to see the barn burning but at the same time, it can be liberating. A new avenue opens up right before our eyes. We see something now that we could not have seen before when the barn was in our way, when we were caught up in our man-made distractions.

We awaken in consciousness and can now see what is really important in life. What seemed a catastrophe becomes a blessing.

Our challenge is to look for the good in everything for in everything, the good can be found if we look for it. We are here to keep our eye focused on the moon—on Spirit—which will give us comfort in all situations always and forever.

Affirmation:

I choose to see Spirit in every situation! By that, I am drawn into the light!

Bein' Alive!

People say that what we're all seeking is a meaning for life. I don't think that's what we're really seeking. I think that what we're seeking is an experience of being alive.

Joseph Campbell

Every time I read Campbell's quote, I feel a great resonance with his words. Yes, being alive is what it is all about. How wonderful to be conscious in this experience called life! We can breathe into the very experience of our aliveness. I'm alive when I'm eager for each new day. I'm alive when I'm excited about the infinite possibilities before me. I'm alive when I let go of my resistance and fear and say "yes" to the next evolution of my existence. I'm alive when I realize how the universe conspires on my behalf as it presents miracle after miracle.

I love that in each moment, we are made brand new, never the same, always becoming more of our true, authentic selves. In that sacred journey is our aliveness. We are a perfect creation of God. Just as the acorn with the proper soil and nutrients becomes the mighty oak, we are here to grow and expand into the dynamic, powerful beings we've come here to be. To do that, we must be willing to move past some old ideas of who we are and what we are capable of in order to accept the bounty that awaits us. There is nothing in the way of our becoming except ourselves, and the universe is here to support us in every way.

Simply, we are here to remove all the barriers to our loving, and when we do that, we become Love Itself. Bein' alive… that's what it feels like! Now I know what it means to be free.

Affirmation:

I'm free to soar as Love Itself!

Life 101: The Learning Laboratory

When you realize that everything springs only from yourself, you will learn both peace and joy.

The Dalai Lama

And all things, whatsoever ye shall ask in prayer, believing, ye shall receive.

Holy Bible, Matthew 21:22

For so many of us, we have thought that life was about getting the goods—the job, the money, the man or woman, the home, the fame, the glory. Now I realize that life was and is never about the "stuff." Life is about the learning along the way, and the learning is what finally gets us to the peace, joy, freedom, love and abundance that we always thought the "stuff" would provide.

Now that's something to think about, isn't it? It's kind of backwards to the way we were taught. In other words, it's what happens to you in your experience during the ups and downs of life, the information gleaned, the new awareness derived, and the choices you make that have the potential to bring you what you've always wanted. It's what you learn along the way and what you then choose to do with what you learn.

We are all on a spiritual soul journey whether we know it or not. The more we learn about understanding, forgiveness, compassion and love, the freer we become. We begin to see it was never about the "stuff." We can be happy even before we have the goods. Once we are living from the fullness of our divine essence, it's that very fullness we desire more of and then the goods flow to us with ease and grace.

It's never too late to take serious thought about our priorities in life. We can open up instantly to our divine potential and set ourselves free from worry and fear. We can truly live and love fearlessly with an undefended heart.

Affirmation:

I am the creator of my good and I am fearless in my living.

The Gift

I am the resurrection and the life; he that believeth in me, though he were dead, yet shall he live.

Holy Bible, St. John: 11:25

His destiny was to be our teacher. What can we learn from the life of Jesus? He was Jesus of Nazareth, son of Mary and, according to the present-day Christian belief, the Savior of mankind. In our teaching, however, Jesus represents the "I" in humankind, the Christ Presence, the embodied Spirit raised to divine understanding and power.

His story tells us that he faced the trials, tribulations and temptations of every man in his earth walk without falling under the influence of evil. We are to look to his life as an example and bring out the Christ Presence in ourselves. We are to accept the truth of our being and to live that truth in thought, word and deed. The Christ is the man that God created, the perfect-idea man and the true self of all of us. Jesus Christ was the Christ self brought forth into perfect expression and manifestation.

We are told to have "this mind in you which was in Christ Jesus" which implies that we can all demonstrate as Jesus did. This requires careful training of our thoughts. It seems an almost superhuman attainment, and it is. The human has to be put away and the divine expressed in its place. The human is transient and fallible; the divine is permanent and infallible. The temptation of Jesus took place within himself so we can see that the place of overcoming is within our own consciousness.

We can resurrect our body just as Jesus resurrected his. We resurrect our body by putting a new mind into it—the mind of Spirit. "Be ye transformed by the renewing of your mind." May we find that place within us of perfect peace and love. May we spread the joy that is our true nature.

Affirmation:

This day and every day, I strive to be more loving in my heart!

One Year to Live

Most of us live half-unborn.

Stephen Levine, *A Year to Live*

This month I am celebrating my own renewal. It appears that I am in a constant state of renewal and expansion. Stephen Levine's words are powerful words spoken. "Most of us live half-unborn." He says when people hear that they are dying, that something breaks free in them. They no longer fear living—in fact, they begin to live as never before. He suggests that we don't have to get a prognosis of our imminent death to really begin living. We can do it now.

I suggest that we open up to our own great life as never before. For all the things you've been putting off "until the right time," the time is now. I'm inviting you to soar! Who would I be without my story? Who would I be without the fear that's been running my life? Who would I be if I were to give my best to the world, and what untold joys might come back to me as a result?

We are here to sing our song, to love as we have never loved before, to dance as though no one is watching and to celebrate our existence here on this physical plane as though we did have only one year left. We are not dying. The truth is we are dying to live. I say why not now? Now is the perfect time to stretch your wings and fly! The Source of all Life supports you in your own becoming.

The utter joy of living and loving fearlessly is awaiting your willingness to step into it. If we do that, this year can become the happiest year of all.

Affirmation:

I joyously celebrate my own becoming! I am fearless in my living!

The Undefended Heart

As God's beloved, I live in bliss knowing that my soul is never separated from Him, for I learn to know Her in all that I see. God dissolved my mind, my separation. I cannot describe now my intimacy with Him.

St. Teresa of Avila

Whatever the question, LOVE is the answer. How can I see this situation beyond fear? How can I live fearlessly? How can I take the action I need to take and still stay in my loving? The truth is, you can.

It is in loving and honoring the Self that we become very clear about how to love and honor another. It is not a place of weakness or selfishness, but rather a place of great power, clarity, integrity and intention. It is YOU deciding you are tired of living with half a heart….tired of half-hearted actions and half-hearted words. It is YOU stripped from the illusions of the story you've been telling about your life. It is the magnificent YOU that has always been worthy and been enough. It is YOU deciding to remove the blocks around your heart so you can actually breathe. It is YOU in that very breath discovering that you have set yourself free in your willingness to live with an undefended heart. Ah, the freedom! It's so simple. I am here. I am open and available. I am clear. I am undefended in my heart, yet ironically, the most powerful and fearless I've ever been.

So where are you? Still protecting yourself from what? Give it up. It was never YOU. It was never real. No matter the question, LOVE is the only answer. I love me and I love you (there is only ONE) and in that is my greatest power. In that is my greatest freedom. In that is my greatest joy.

Affirmation:

I AM. I AM all I need to be.

Living Your Extraordinary Life

When you break through in your mind, believing you can rise higher and overcome obstacles, then God will unleash the power within that will enable you to go beyond the ordinary into the extraordinary life you were designed to live.

Joel Osteen, *Break Out!*

As Joel says we are here to live extraordinary lives, not just ordinary lives. The only thing holding us back is our own reluctance to claim the fullness of our good. We ask for a thimble full when in reality we can have a barn full or even more. It is about minding our minds, however, and that takes some amount of discipline.

Generally, my feelings give me a clue as to what I'm thinking. In my effort to stay on the "high flying disk" as Abraham-Hicks would say (meaning staying in the high vibration of positive energy), I sometimes find myself criticizing my mind for thinking negative thoughts, almost making of my mind the enemy. I realize that is not a beneficial approach. I'm not here to fight against my own mind or, for that matter, any aspect of my being. A gentler approach is to say to myself that I am the guardian of Divine Mind. My mind is an aspect of the One Mind, the Mind of God. I'm not here to resist or fight against anything—even my own negative thoughts or the illusions of the past.

The idea that I am the guardian of the Divine Mind, which is my mind, brings peace to my heart and easy access to loving thoughts that enrich and expand my life. Being the guardian of my mind puts me in a more protective, peaceful stance. As I let go of my resistance, the love which is the hub of my life has an opportunity to flourish. Negativity then has no power over me because I remember in that moment that I am the guardian of Divine Mind, that I have access to the Kingdom of God, and that I am here to live an extraordinary life.

Affirmation:

There is a power within me that I can access. I am the guardian of Divine Mind.

Divine Resurrection

Man, by thinking, can bring into his experience whatever he desires — if he thinks correctly, and becomes a living embodiment of his thoughts.

Ernest Holmes, *The Science of Mind*

The great resurrection is happening within. We move into the becoming and we do it trusting that we are always expanding into the greater. It happens through our dedication to the inner work. We pray, we meditate, we study, we trust that there is a power greater than we are that loves us and supports us unfailingly. We strive to see the better, truer view in all our interactions. We strive to see the perfection even in the imperfections. We forgive because we can. Being in conflict with even one person strains our relations with everyone.

What we perceive as being outside of ourselves is really our own internal creation. Whatever happened yesterday or last year or forty years ago can be forgiven in an instant. Forgiveness is a choice and we can make it today. The absence of peace knows no bounds, and we are here to experience the great peace within, the great love within, the great wisdom within. We are here in this physical dimension to experience the Divine Resurrection into the light of our own being. That was the wonderful message Jesus gave to us. We can overcome all.

It's our lesson to learn, and then practice, in every opportunity that's available, acceptance of ourselves. When we do, we'll begin to feel total acceptance of others too. When that happens, we are free in a whole new way. We live from the I AM, the Christ Presence within and we celebrate our oneness with everyone and everything.

Affirmation:

Who I see is who I AM today!

A Reason and a Season for All Things

Be a light unto yourself.

The Buddha

Have you ever considered that everyone who comes into your life is there for a reason? When we begin to see everyone as the teacher we've been waiting for, it sheds a whole new light on our experience. Ah….we can say this one, or this experience, is here to teach me something about myself. It doesn't mean we won't feel the barbs, attack and insults, but it gives us a whole new perspective. What am I to learn about myself in the face of this situation? What does the insult I feel tell me about myself? It doesn't mean I won't feel the hurt inside myself, but it is the great gift given to me in order that I might learn my next great lesson. Believe it or not, this person or experience is here to help me on my journey to awakening to the divine essence and the love within me.

Nothing and no one has the power to control us or destroy us. We may resist the lessons we are here to learn; it takes us whatever season it takes to learn the lesson, but it gives us another way of seeing a situation. Gratefully, in addition, our new perspective automatically brings us back into our own power. We learn to be more detached from the particulars of the situation and able then to focus on healing that part of us that has been in the dark for so long.

This is the nature of this loving universe in which we live—always giving us exactly what we need at exactly the right time. I am so grateful for all my teachers throughout my life who have helped remind me of the truth of my being!

Affirmation:

I will accept today's journey as the one I'm ready for. I will make a contribution on behalf of love today.

Divine Inspiration

I have learned silence from the talkative, tolerance from the intolerant, and kindness from the unkind. Yet, strange, I am ungrateful to these teachers.

Kahlil Gibran

It would be nice if everyone thought just like us and agreed with our opinions. That would make life easier and we wouldn't have to work our judgment muscle so much. That's not the way it is, however; and there are those people in our lives who push our buttons in a big way. Sometimes we can get away from them and sometimes, at least for now, it appears they are here to stay. I've learned to call them my current and best teachers, and I'm discovering the power of love if I can pay undistractable attention to staying in it no matter what.

I've watched anger and upset dissolve in an instant when there is nothing to push against. When I stay in my loving, anything unlike it dissolves. Jesus called it nonresistance. That is the secret weapon—love with nonresistance. We have heard so often "what you resist persists." Resist not. Be still in your loving. When others are angry and upset, they can't hear you anyway. Be still. Listen. Do not engage energetically. This all sounds so good and yet, we are human, and it isn't always so easy to do.

We all want to be loved but we have not been taught how to love well. I think it is time for the great suffering from lack of love to end on the planet. The more we practice living in love—"What would love do here?"—the easier it becomes. It is the perfect tool to have in your conscious living tool kit. When we become love and cease having anything to prove, we are finally and exquisitely free!

Affirmation:

Today I reach out with love. I send love to people everywhere. I know that as I love, I am loved.

Who Am I?

What each must seek in his life… is something out of his own unique potentiality for experience, something that never has been and never could have been experienced by anyone else.

Joseph Campbell

We decide who we are going to be in each and every moment. We're responsible for cultivating the kind of personalities we have every minute we're present in this world. We can decide if we want to continue to be argumentative, judgmental, or unkind. We can decide if we want to be a more understanding and compassionate person. Yet sometimes I think we believe that this is the way we are and we, and others, just have to live with it. Well, that is not the case. We have choice in the matter, and that is what becoming conscious is all about. We realize that if we want less conflict in our lives then we need to be less argumentative. If we want to be appreciated more than we are, then we need to find more to appreciate in other people and the world around us. We have dominion over our experience.

This is a radical thought to one who always sees the glass half empty or who sees the negative in everything and everyone. It's so much easier to blame the world for our disappointments.

The big question is whether you want to change. How much would you like to experience a more loving, joy-filled life? It's up to you. No one else can do it for you. Decide that you are willing to see the world differently and then watch as it comes to pass.

Affirmation:

I am willing to be a more loving, compassionate and understanding person. I am willing to be happy.

I am the Truth, the Way and the Life

You shall be free indeed when your days are not without a care nor your nights without a want and a grief, but rather when these things girdle your life and yet you rise above them naked and unbound.

Kahlil Gibran

The unconditional love of God is flowing through and as us in every moment of every day. It is we who put the conditions on that beautiful unconditional love. We do that by judging ourselves or others, by resisting the very thing we say we want, by ideas of lack and limitation, by focusing on the negatives rather than the positives in our lives. Our active minds get in the way of experiencing this incredible love seeking to express fully through and as us. We doubt ourselves, restrict ourselves and deny the very thing we say we want.

To experience this great gift of love that is sourcing through and as us in every moment, we must yield and surrender into it. We must turn off the negative mind chatter and feed our minds a steady flow of beautiful declarations of peace, love, joy, abundance, light, and all the good things that we wish to experience. We must reprogram our minds to see only good and infinite possibility. Then we must be in a constant state of gratitude, which will not be hard because the more we program our minds to see only good, the more good we will experience.

This is successful, joyous living. This is the recipe for having what you want in life. It works every time. Is it easy? No, not for those of us who have spent a great deal of time living in doubt, fear, worry and confusion. But it is the formula for success in this physical world. We chose this incarnation to practice this very truth. So do not waste your life denying the love of God. Take up your bed and walk. You will be supported in ways unimaginable by the very Source which created you.

Affirmation:

I am the unconditional love of God. I allow that love to flow through and as me!

Staying Calm When the River's Rising

Mastering others is strength. Mastering yourself is true power.

Lao-Tzu

Staying calm when the river's rising—that's the key. We live in a world of ups and downs and inside outs… births, deaths, illness and miracle healings, all happening simultaneously. This is the human condition. Our spiritual work does not make us immune from that. What it does do is make the living easier. It enables us to see the greater Truth when those around us cannot see it. It provides an inner strength and resilience that can and will weather any storm. It enables us to see infinite possibility when others see despair. It fortifies us in clear knowing when others are ready to give up. It reminds us of our loving compassionate nature when we are ready to give up. It calms us in the storm and sustains us in the peace.

Relying on Divine Spirit, we can stay calm when the river's rising—that's how we become a beneficial presence. It's not about fighting against anything. It's not about resisting anything. It's about living from the inside out. It's about living from the Divine Knower within. If I can see the good, I can help someone else see it. If I can believe in the healing, someone else can begin to believe it.

That's our main job—to stay in our loving and it is not easy because we get triggered when someone does something or says something that touches an unhealed place inside of us. We do our spiritual work to heal those places so that we may stay anchored in truth no matter what is coming our way.

The river may rise, but I shall not be moved. I remember who I am and whose I am. Because of that, I can see you clearly too.

Affirmation:

I trust myself completely to say and do the right thing. My heart is pure!

It's All Sacred!

If God said, Rumi, pay homage to everything that has helped you enter my arms, there would not be one experience of my life, not one thought, not one feeling, not any act, I would not bow to.

Jalaludin Rumi (1207-1273)

In a meditation recently I recalled myself as a young girl, lying on my belly watching red ants go in and out of an ant hill. In that moment, I saw the wonder, innocence and beauty of my childhood. I saw how many times I was happy and carefree and all the wonderful experiences that I had. It surprised me to be seeing my youth in such a positive light. The truth was that other things happened to me in my youth which were not beautiful. Regretfully, those were the things that I chose to spend the majority of my life focusing upon.

In my willingness to forgive and let go of all that seemed hurtful and destructive to me at the time, I can now look back on my life from a new perspective and see all the many blessings. The negative experiences no longer have power over me. Rumi said it so beautifully...everything is sacred. In our awakening, we remember who we are as precious innocence. We claim our divinity. We embrace everything and everyone as part of the whole and we can see, perhaps for the first time, our complete life as a masterpiece.

Now I see my past as precious and exciting and filled with possibility and I claim that for my present and for my future as well. As Rumi so beautifully says "there is no experience of my life, not one thought, not one feeling, not any act I would not bow to." All of it brought me to my Self... God, and for that, I am forever grateful.

Affirmation:

My whole life is a blessing and I am grateful!

Gratitude as a Way of Life

Thanksgiving is one of the highest forms of prayer.

Emmet Fox

Every day I thank God for all I've been given and every day, more comes to me. That is because gratitude is an open and receptive state of being. The vibration is high and the vision is sharp. The world is a more beautiful place because I'm in a more beautiful place.

As I move into another great expression in my life...always more, never less...I realize that in this life I'm always moving from one blessing to another. No matter what circumstance we are in, there is a blessing in it when we chose to see it that way. Maybe it is an opportunity to learn something more about ourselves that we could not possibly have learned any other way.

The great joy is the awareness that we are constantly being guided and directed to exactly the next right thing for us to do. Sometimes it takes great courage to take the leap but when we do, we are rewarded mightily. A greater expression unfolds within us of light, love, peace and joy. Suddenly we realize that the place we were standing before was absolutely necessary for us to step into this greater expression.

This is the nature of our spiritual journey on the planet… constant evolution, constant growth, becoming more like our True Self all the time. Ultimately, we see through the eyes of Love and witness it everywhere because Love is who we are. May you always experience your life's journey as one great ongoing blessing and be thankful for it!

Affirmation:

I boldly and courageously move into the next expression of my life knowing that I'm becoming more, never less. Love shows Its face as me and I am grateful!

EPILOGUE

I found the very early hours of day to be the best time to compose many of these writings. My mind was fresh and free at that time from the thousands of thoughts that pass through daily.

Every time I wrote one of these inspirations, I was in discovery of a new way of seeing a situation and my part in it, and hence a new way of being in the world.

I am in gratitude that somewhere in the deepest part of me, an answer always appeared that would deliver me into greater understanding and compassion. This inner wisdom is part of our innate nature. We must learn to trust that it is within us and that ultimately we can trust ourselves to know what we need to know when we need to know it. The journey is sweet and profound and yes, life is worth living and worth living to its fullest.

ACKNOWLEDGMENTS

My great gratitude goes to Viki King, Rev. Mary Miller, Gerry Stanek, and Joyce Huntington Stanek, each of whom helped me in a unique way in the creation of this book.

ABOUT THE AUTHOR

Karen Wylie is a wisdom holder and teacher of truth principles for living a joyous and abundant life. She is also an ordained minister from the Agape International Spiritual Center in Culver City, California. She is an agent for transformation, helping others develop their inner awareness and confidence. Currently in her global work, she writes, facilitates workshops and retreats, provides private consultations, spiritual counseling, and ceremonies of all kinds, leads sacred journeys and speaks to communities throughout the country. She inspires her audiences to express their innate spiritual nature in all areas of their lives through authentic living.

Karen became licensed as a minister upon her 2008 graduation from the University of Transformational Studies and Leadership at the Agape International Spiritual Center under the direction of Michael Bernard Beckwith. Her credentials also include a B.A. in Psychology from UCLA, becoming a licensed Spiritual Counselor in 1994 at Agape, and obtaining a Master's Degree in Spiritual Psychology from the University of Santa Monica in 2001. Upon her ministerial graduation in 2008, from June 2009 to October 2013, Karen served as Spiritual Director of the Symphony of Life Spiritual Center in Ojai, California. She was ordained on June 24, 2012, by Michael Bernard Beckwith. As an active member of Agape for twenty years, she served primarily in the Education and Pastoral Care Ministries. She is also licensed as a practitioner with Centers for Spiritual Living and has held her license there since 1994. After a year of ministerial training, in 2004, she "retired" from her profession as an Employee Benefits Specialist and spent two-plus years traveling around the world visiting sacred sites and indigenous peoples.

A prolific writer, she is a contributor to various inspirational publications, including Inner Visions magazine of the Agape International Spiritual Center, and the Science of Mind magazine.

An enthusiastic traveler and guide, Karen leads groups on sacred journeys to sites throughout the world, including the House of Mary and the ancient city of Ephesus in Turkey, the temples and major sites of Egypt, swimming with the dolphins in the wild in Hawaii, facilitating sacred ceremonies in Sedona, Arizona, and exploring and discovering the spirit of Florence, Siena, and Assisi, Italy.

Karen is a lover of life and a spiritual adventurer. As a highly intuitive and passionate teacher of truth, Karen lives and loves fearlessly and empowers others to do the same.

For more information, go to **www.karenswylie.com**

Made in the USA
Middletown, DE
07 August 2015